YOUR PERSONAL

ASTROLOGY

PLANNER

LEO
2010

YOUR PERSONAL

ASTROLOGY

PLANNER

LEO
2010

RICK LEVINE **& JEFF** JAWER

STERLING

New York / London
www.sterlingpublishing.com

STERLING and the distinctive Sterling logo are registered
trademarks of Sterling Publishing Co., Inc.

2 4 6 8 10 9 7 5 3 1

Published by Sterling Publishing Co., Inc.
387 Park Avenue South, New York, NY 10016
© 2009 Sterling Publishing Co., Inc.
Text © 2009 Rick Levine and Jeff Jawer
Distributed in Canada by Sterling Publishing
c/o Canadian Manda Group, 165 Dufferin Street,
Toronto, Ontario, Canada M6K 3H6
Distributed in the United Kingdom by GMC Distribution Services
Castle Place, 166 High Street, Lewes, East Sussex, England BN7 1XU
Distributed in Australia by Capricorn Link (Australia) Pty. Ltd.
P.O. Box 704, Windsor, NSW 2756, Australia

Manufactured in the United States of America
All rights reserved

Sterling ISBN 978-1-4027-6407-3

For information about custom editions, special sales, premium and
corporate purchases, please contact Sterling Special Sales
Department at 800-805-5489 or
specialsales@sterlingpublishing.com.

TABLE OF CONTENTS

Introduction   7
Moon Charts   11

CHAPTER I: ASTROLOGY, YOU & THE WORLD   15

**CHAPTER 2: LEO AUGUST–DECEMBER   35
            2009 OVERVIEW**

CHAPTER 3: 2010 HOROSCOPE   46

APPENDIXES
2010 Month-at-a-Glance Astrocalendar   131
Famous Leos   143
Leo in Love   145
Author Biographies   158
Acknowledgments   159

THE PURPOSE OF THIS BOOK

The more you learn about yourself, the better able you are to wisely use the energies in your life. For more than 3,000 years, astrology has been the sharpest tool in the box for describing the human condition. Used by virtually every culture on the planet, astrology continues to serve as a link between individual lives and planetary cycles. We gain valuable insights into personal issues with a birth chart, and can plot the patterns of the year ahead in meaningful ways for individuals as well as groups. You share your sun sign with eight percent of humanity. Clearly, you're not all going to have the same day, even if the basic astrological cycles are the same. Your individual circumstances, the specific factors of your entire birth chart, and your own free will help you write your unique story.

The purpose of this book is to describe the energies of the Sun, Moon, and planets for the year ahead and help you create your future, rather than being a victim of it. We aim to facilitate your journey by showing you the turns ahead in the road of life and hopefully the best ways to navigate them.

YOU ARE THE STAR
OF YOUR LIFE

It is not our goal to simply predict events. Rather, we are reporting the planetary energies—the cosmic weather in which you are living—so that you understand these conditions and know how to use them most effectively.

The power, though, isn't in the stars, but in your mind, your heart, and the choices that you make every day. Regardless of how strongly you are buffeted by the winds of change or bored by stagnation, you have many ways to view any situation. Learning about the energies of the Sun, Moon, and planets will both sharpen and widen your perspective, thereby giving you additional choices.

The language of astrology is a gift of awareness, not a rigid set of rules. It works best when blended with common sense, intuition, and self-trust. This is your life, and no one knows how to live it as well as you. Take what you need from this book and leave the rest. Although the planets set the stage for the year ahead, you're the writer, director, and star of your life and you can play the part in whatever way you choose. *Your Personal Astrology Planner* uses information about your sun sign to give you a better understanding of how the planetary waves will wash upon your shore. We each navigate our lives through time, and each moment has unique qualities. Astrology gives us the ability to describe the constantly changing timescape. For example, if you know the trajectory and the speed of an approaching storm, you can choose to delay a leisurely afternoon sail on the bay, thus avoiding an unpleasant situation.

By reading this book, you can improve your ability to align with the cosmic weather, the larger patterns that affect you day to day. You can become more effective by aligning with the cosmos and cocreating the year ahead with a better understanding of the energies around you.

Astrology doesn't provide quick fixes to life's complex issues. It doesn't offer neatly packed black-and-white answers in a world filled with an infinite variety of shapes and colors. It can, however, give you a much clearer picture of the invisible forces influencing your life.

ENERGY & EVENTS

Two sailboats can face the same gale yet travel in opposite directions as a result of how the sails are positioned. Similarly, how you respond to the energy of a particular set of circumstances may be more responsible for your fate than the given situation itself. We delineate the energetic winds for your year ahead, but your attitude shapes the unfolding events, and your responses alter your destiny.

This book emphasizes the positive, not because all is good, but because astrology shows us ways to transform even the power of a storm into beneficial results. Empowerment comes from learning to see the invisible energy patterns that impact the visible landscape as you fill in the details of your story every day on this spinning planet, orbited by the Moon, lit by the Sun, and colored by the nuances of the planets.

You are a unique point in an infinite galaxy of unlimited possibilities, and the choices that you make have consequences. So use this book in a most magical way to consciously improve your life.

MOON CHARTS

2010 NEW MOONS

Each New Moon marks the beginning of a cycle. In general, this is the best time to plant seeds for future growth. Use the days preceeding the New Moon to finish old business prior to starting what comes next. The focused mind can be quite sharp during this phase. Harness the potential of the New Moon by stating your intentions—out loud or in writing—for the weeks ahead. Hold these goals in your mind; help them grow to fruition through conscious actions as the Moon gains light during the following two weeks. In the chart below, the dates and times refer to when the Moon and Sun align in each zodiac sign (see p16), initiating a new lunar cycle.

DATE	TIME	SIGN
January 15	2:11 AM EST	Capricorn (ECLIPSE)
February 13	9:51 PM EST	Aquarius
March 15	5:01 PM EDT	Pisces
April 14	8:28 AM EDT	Aries
May 13	9:04 PM EDT	Taurus
June 12	7:14 AM EDT	Gemini
July 11	3:40 PM EDT	Cancer (ECLIPSE)
August 9	11:08 PM EDT	Leo
September 8	6:29 AM EDT	Virgo
October 7	2:44 PM EDT	Libra
November 6	12:51 AM EDT	Scorpio
December 5	12:35 PM EST	Sagittarius

2010 FULL MOONS

The Full Moon reflects the light of the Sun as subjective feelings reflect the objective events of the day. Dreams seem bigger; moods feel stronger. The emotional waters run with deeper currents. This is the phase of culmination, a turning point in the energetic cycle. Now it's time to listen to the inner voices. Rather than starting new projects, the two weeks after the Full Moon are when we complete what we can and slow our outward expressions in anticipation of the next New Moon. In this chart, the dates and times refer to when the moon is opposite the sun in each zodiac sign, marking the emotional peak of each lunar cycle.

DATE	TIME	SIGN
January 30	1:17 AM EST	Leo
February 28	11:37 AM EST	Virgo
March 29	10:25 PM EDT	Libra
April 28	8:18 AM EDT	Scorpio
May 27	7:07 PM EDT	Sagittarius
June 26	7:30 AM EDT	Capricorn **(ECLIPSE)**
July 25	9:36 PM EDT	Aquarius
August 24	1:04 PM EDT	Pisces
September 23	5:17 AM EDT	Aries
October 22	9:36 PM EDT	Aries
November 21	12:27 PM EST	Taurus
December 21	3:13 AM EST	Gemini **(ECLIPSE)**

ASTROLOGY, YOU & THE WORLD

WELCOME TO YOUR SUN SIGN

The Sun, Moon, and Earth and all the planets
lie within a plane called the **ecliptic** and move
through a narrow band of stars made up by
12 constellations called the **zodiac**. The Earth
revolves around the Sun once a year, but from
our point of view, it appears that the Sun moves
through each sign of the zodiac for one month.
There are 12 months and astrologically there are
12 signs. The astrological months, however, do
not match our calendar, and start between the
19th and 23rd of each month. Everyone is born
to an astrological month, like being born in a
room with a particular perspective of the world.
Knowing your sun sign provides useful information
about your personality and your future, but for a
more detailed astrological analysis, a full birth
chart calculation based on your precise date,
time, and place of birth is necessary. Get your
complete birth chart online at:

http://www.tarot.com/astrology/astroprofile

This book is about your zodiac sign. Your Sun is in the fire sign of proud Leo, the Lion. Your greatest strength is your generosity in love, but you usually need to be appreciated and loved in return. When insecure, you aggressively seek attention. You can be like a dramatically roaring and posturing male Lion, or a quieter Lioness relentlessly getting on with her business of hunting and tending her cubs. Either way, you're an intense, fun-loving, spirited force of nature.

THE PLANETS

We refer to the Sun and Moon as planets. Don't worry; we do know about modern astronomy. Although the Sun is really a star and the Moon is a satellite, they are called planets for astrological purposes. The astrological planets are the Sun, the Moon, Mercury, Venus, Mars, Jupiter, Saturn, Chiron, Uranus, Neptune, and Pluto.

Your sun sign is the most obvious astrological placement, for the Sun returns to the same sign every year. But at the same time, the Moon is orbiting the Earth, changing signs every two and a third days. Mercury, Venus, and Mars each move

through a sign in a few weeks to a few months.
Jupiter spends a whole year in a sign—and Pluto
visits a sign for up to 30 years! The ever-changing
positions of the planets alter the energetic terrain
through which we travel. The planets are symbols;
each has a particular range of meanings. For
example, Venus is the goddess of love, but it really
symbolizes beauty in a spectrum of experiences.
Venus can represent romantic love, sensuality, the
arts, or good food. It activates anything that we
value, including personal possessions and even
money. To our ancestors, the planets actually
animated life on Earth. In this way of thinking, every
beautiful flower contains the essence of Venus.

Each sign has a natural affinity to an individual
planet, and as this planet moves through the sky, it
sends messages of particular interest to people born
under that sign. Our home star, the Sun, is your
key or ruling planet, illuminating your life with dig-
nity, courage, and willpower. As the Sun moves
through your chart, it lights up the corresponding
areas of your life, drives you to express yourself,
and bestows creativity, charisma, and confidence
upon you. Planets can be described by many different words, for the mythology of each is a rich

tapestry. In this book we use a variety of words when talking about each planet in order to convey the most applicable meaning. The table below describes a few keywords for each planet, including the Sun and Moon.

PLANET	SYMBOL	KEYWORDS
Sun	☉	Consciousness, Will, Vitality
Moon	☽	Subconscious, Emotions, Habits
Mercury	☿	Communication, Thoughts, Transportation
Venus	♀	Desire, Love, Money, Values
Mars	♂	Action, Physical Energy, Drive
Jupiter	♃	Expansion, Growth, Optimism
Saturn	♄	Contraction, Maturity, Responsibility
Chiron	⚷	Healing, Pain, Subversion
Uranus	♅	Awakening, Unpredictable, Inventive
Neptune	♆	Imagination, Spirituality, Confusion
Pluto	♇	Passion, Intensity, Regeneration

HOUSES

Just as planets move through the signs of the zodiac, they also move through the houses in an individual chart. The 12 houses correspond to the 12 signs, but are individualized, based upon your

sign. In this book we use Solar Houses, which place
your sun sign in your 1st House. Therefore, when
a planet enters a new sign it also enters a new
house. If you know your exact time of birth, the
rising sign determines the 1st House. You can
learn your rising sign by entering your birth date at:
   http://www.tarot.com/astrology/astroprofile

HOUSE	SIGN	KEYWORDS
1st House	Aries	Self, Appearance, Personality
2nd House	Taurus	Possessions, Values, Self-Worth
3rd House	Gemini	Communication, Siblings, Short Trips
4th House	Cancer	Home, Family, Roots
5th House	Leo	Love, Romance, Children, Play
6th House	Virgo	Work, Health, Daily Routines
7th House	Libra	Marriage, Relationships, Business Partners
8th House	Scorpio	Intimacy, Transformation, Shared Resources
9th House	Sagittarius	Travel, Higher Education, Philosophy
10th House	Capricorn	Career, Community, Ambition
11th House	Aquarius	Groups and Friends, Associations, Social Ideals
12th House	Pisces	Imagination, Spirituality, Secret Activities

ASPECTS

As the planets move through the sky in their various cycles, they form ever-changing angles with one another. Certain angles create significant geometric shapes. So, when two planets are 90 degrees apart, they conform to a square; 60 degrees of separation conforms to a sextile, or six-pointed star. Planets create **aspects** when they're at these special angles. Aspects explain how the individual symbolism of pairs of planets combine into an energetic pattern.

ASPECT	DEGREES	KEYWORDS
Conjunction	0	Compression, Blending, Focus
Opposition	180	Tension, Awareness, Balance
Trine	120	Harmony, Free-Flowing, Ease
Square	90	Resistance, Stress, Dynamic Conflict
Quintile	72	Creativity, Metaphysical, Magic
Sextile	60	Support, Intelligent, Activating
Quincunx	150	Irritation, Annoyance, Adjustment

2010 GENERAL FORECAST:
THE INDIVIDUAL AND THE COLLECTIVE

Astrology works for individuals, groups, and even for humanity as a whole. You will have your own story in 2010, but it will unfold among nearly seven billion other tales of human experience. We are each unique, yet our lives touch one another; our destinies are woven together by weather and war, by the economy, science, music, politics, religion, and all the other threads of life on planet Earth. We make personal choices every day, yet great events are beyond the control of anyone. When a town is flooded, it affects everyone, yet personal astrology patterns will describe the specific response of each person. Our existence is both an individual and a collective experience.

We are living in a time when the tools of self-awareness fill books, TV and radio shows, Web sites, podcasts, newspapers, and DVDs, and we benefit greatly from them. Yet despite of all this wisdom, conflicts cause enormous suffering every day. Understanding personal issues is a powerful means for increasing happiness, but knowledge of our collective issues is equally important for our safety, sanity, and well-being. This astrological look at the major trends and planetary patterns for 2010 provides a framework for comprehending the potentials and challenges we face together, so that we can advance with tolerance and respect as a community and fulfill our potential as individuals.

The astrological events used for this forecast are the transits of major planets Jupiter and Saturn, the retrograde cycles of Mercury, and the eclipses of the Sun and the Moon.

A NOTE ABOUT DATES IN THIS BOOK

All events are based upon the Eastern Time Zone of the United States. Because of local time differences, an event occurring just a few minutes after midnight in the East will actually happen the prior day in the rest of the country. Although the key dates are the exact dates of any particular alignment, some of you are so ready for certain things to happen that you can react to a transit a day or two before it is exact. And sometimes you can be so entrenched in habits or unwilling to change that you may not notice the effects right away. Allow extra time around each key date to feel the impact of any event.

JUPITER IN PISCES:
WILD WAVES OF CHANGE
January 17, 2010–June 6, 2010
September 9, 2010–January 22, 2011

Jupiter, the planet of expansion, reconnects us with our
spiritual roots in its watery home sign of Pisces.
Knowledge is no longer an intellectual abstraction; it is
a living experience that comes from our connection to
the cosmos. Imagination is stronger now as the limits
of logic are dissolved in the boundless waters of intuition, which seem to reveal answers to all life's ques-
tions. The great gift of Jupiter in Pisces is that wisdom
is equally available to everyone. The challenge, though,
is connecting the grand vision that inspires us with the
specific steps required to turn it into reality.
Fortunately, Jupiter's foray into action-oriented Aries
provides the fire to set concepts into motion.

JUPITER IN ARIES:
A GLIMPSE OF THE FUTURE
June 6, 2010–September 9, 2010
January 22, 2011–June 4, 2011

A new day dawns with farseeing Jupiter in pioneering
Aries. The urge to test ideas on the battlefield of experience amplifies impatience yet rewards individuals
and institutions willing to take risks. Breakthroughs in
energy generation are now possible. Innovations in

education and travel are likely to follow. However, a lack of compromise on ideological matters can increase the potential for conflict. Bold statements and actions provoke rapid responses, reducing the effectiveness of diplomacy. Jupiter's stressful aspects with Saturn, Uranus, and Pluto may pit progressive forces against those who resist change. On the positive side, new ways of seeing ourselves can quickly break down old barriers, allowing our common humanity to overcome the differences of nationality, ideology, religion, gender, and race.

SATURN IN VIRGO:
HEALTHY VIGILANCE
September 2, 2007–October 29, 2009
April 7, 2010–July 21, 2010

Saturn, the planet of boundaries and limitations, takes twenty-nine years to orbit the Sun and pass through all twelve signs of the zodiac. It demands serious responsibility, reveals the work necessary to overcome obstacles, and teaches us how to structure our lives. Saturn thrives on patience and commitment, rewarding well-planned and persistent effort while punishing sloppiness and procrastination with disappointment, delay, and even failure.

Saturn's passage through methodical Virgo is a time to perfect skills, cut waste, and develop healthier habits. Virgo is less interested in unrestrained consumerism than in acquiring useful things. This opens the door to a new era of less conspicuous consumption and shifts the economy away from purchases of SUVs, big homes, and luxury items. Issues relating to impure food and water have already been in the news, with outbreaks of salmonella and E. coli poisoning raising wider concerns about contamination and urging us to improve our diets. Environmental concerns continue to escalate as we approach a critical point in the relationship between humanity and planet Earth. Fortunately, Saturn in exacting Virgo is also excellent for cleaning up unhealthy toxins produced by old technologies and building new ecologically friendly systems for the future.

SATURN IN LIBRA:
SURGE OF DIPLOMACY
October 29, 2009–April 7, 2010
July 21, 2010–October 5, 2012

Saturn's shift into peace-loving Libra marks a new chapter in all kinds of relationships, but there's some tough work to be done before harmony can be achieved. Saturn in Libra marks a time of significant legal changes when the scales of justice are recalibrated. The famous *Brown v. Board of Education* case—critical to reversing segregation in the United States—was launched in 1951 with Saturn in Libra. During this cycle, the legal definition of marriage is under reconsideration as we weigh and balance the spreading acceptance of same-sex marriages against the more traditional approach. The US Fairness Doctrine, which requires broadcasters to present contrasting views regarding controversial issues of public interest, could come up for scrutiny. Even challenges to international treaties governing war and peace can be expected.

When Saturn in Libra functions at its best, cooperation and civility allow diplomacy to flourish as reason replaces force. The need to weigh both sides of any argument can slow personal and public dialogue, yet it's worth the price to build bridges over seemingly impassable chasms. The negative side of Saturn, though, is its potential for rigidity, which can manifest now as a stubborn unwillingness to listen. Resistance to opposing points of view is simply an opportunity to test their worth; only with careful consideration can they be properly evaluated. Responsible individuals and wise leaders recognize the importance of treating others with respect as a foundation for any healthy relationship.

MERCURY RETROGRADES
**December 26, 2009–January 15, 2010 in Capricorn /
April 18–May 11 in Taurus / August 20–September 12
in Virgo / December 10 in Capricorn,
Direct December 30 in Sagittarius**

All true planets appear to move backward from time to time, because we view them from the moving platform of Earth. The most significant retrograde cycles are those of Mercury, the communication planet. Occurring three or four times a year for roughly three weeks at a time, these are periods when difficulties with travel, communication, details, and technical matters are likely.

Although many people think that Mercury's retrograde is negative, you can make this cycle work for you. Because personal and commercial interactions are emphasized, you can actually accomplish more than usual, especially if you stay focused on what needs to be done rather than initiating new projects. Still, you may feel as if you're treading water—or worse, carried backward in an undertow of unfinished business. Worry less about making progress than about the quality of your work. Pay extra attention to all your communication exchanges. Avoiding misunderstandings and omissions is the ideal way to minimize complications. Retrograde Mercury is best used to tie up loose ends as you review, redo, reconsider, and, in general, revisit the past.

This year, all four retrogrades begin in practical earth signs (Capricorn, Taurus, Virgo), challenging us to redefine our material values, ambitions, and methods. Sticking to literal interpretations of reality during these periods can be extremely limiting. We are pushed to question our perceptions and break the forms of recognition and description that bind us to our current ways of seeing and communicating. Intuitive approaches in which the subjective qualities of life take on more importance fill in the gaps where objective analyses fall short.

ECLIPSES
Solar: January 15 and July 11
Lunar: June 26 and December 21

Solar and Lunar Eclipses are special New and Full Moons that indicate significant changes for individuals and groups. They are powerful markers of events with influences that can appear up to three months in advance and last up to six months afterward.

January 15, Solar Eclipse in Capricorn: Fall from Grace

The powerful changes of this eclipse are softened by its close conjunction with gentle Venus. Heads of state—especially female—may fall, but they're likely to land in cushy places with the planet of love and rewards in the picture. A supportive sextile from inventive Uranus encourages alternative forms of leadership and helpful shakeups in large organizations. This eclipse is visible through the middle of China, the southern tip of India, and Central Africa, making its impact stronger in these areas.

June 26, Lunar Eclipse in Capricorn: Sudden Exposure

This Lunar Eclipse is conjunct insatiable Pluto, indicating major issues that threaten safety and security. Abuse of power is likely, especially in traditional institutions that have long resisted reform and exposure to public scrutiny. Toxicity can be a concern with Pluto's presence, perhaps affecting food supplies. The volatile conjunction of Jupiter and Uranus square the eclipse may precipitate rapid changes that unexpectedly undermine the viability of influential organizations. Positively, a healthy purge can restore life to fading companies and failing governments.

July 11, Solar Eclipse in Cancer:
Water Works

The potential for problems is considerable with this Total Eclipse of the Sun conjunct the karmic South Node of the Moon. Water may be threatened by pollution or become threatening itself through storms and flooding. Fortunately, Mars in efficient Virgo forms an intelligent sextile to the eclipse that provides rapid responses whenever corrective action is needed. The vast majority of the path of visibility falls over water in the South Pacific, reducing its area of influence. It does touch the southern tip of South America, where its effects may be more evident.

December 21, Lunar Eclipse in Gemini:
Static on the Line

Tranquility on the home front and travel for the holidays may be disturbed by this Total Lunar Eclipse in the chatty transportation sign of Gemini. Intense Pluto and talkative Mercury oppose the Moon, triggering provocative conversations and communication breakdowns. The Jupiter-Uranus conjunction squares the eclipse, adding another degree of instability that could trigger earthquakes or unusual weather. Still, brilliant ideas can explode from unexpected sources to drastically shift our perceptions and the ways in which we connect with one another.

THE BOTTOM LINE:
SAVE THE HUMANS

All the talk about transformational shifts in 2012 at the supposed end of the Mayan calendar overlooks the incredible planetary forces that will reshape the future of humanity this year. Undoubtedly there will be major changes during slow-moving Uranus-Pluto squares of 2012–2015, reawakening the energy of the mid-1960s when revolutionary Uranus conjoined evolutionary Pluto. But we don't need to wait until then—when it may be too late—to start the work that so desperately needs to be done. The formative forces of the outer planets aligning at the beginning of the cardinal signs in 2010 suggest that the new era is opening now. The movements of expansive Jupiter and structuring Saturn from season-ending mutable signs where old energy is released to the initiating signs of Aries and Libra are enough by themselves to tell the tale of an emerging new world order.

Our least viable option, and most unlikely scenario, is standing still in a futile attempt to maintain the status quo. The year 2010 is not one of stagnation; it's a year when the slow simmer of unresolved issues boils over and demands our attention. The degree of stress is high, yet the potential for finally making the structural changes and sacrifices necessary to save humanity does exist. This is, happily, not some dreary trudge toward inevitable failure, but a turning point when the

pressure of physical stress crosses with the genius
of human potential to take us on a healthier and more
hopeful path to the future.

Remember that all these astrological events are
part of the general cosmic weather of the year, but will
affect us each differently based on our individual
astrological signs.

LEO
AUGUST–DECEMBER
2009 OVERVIEW

RELATIONSHIP DILEMMA

It's time for summer play . . . but you also have your share of work to do this month. The Sun remains in your sign until **August 22**, illuminating recent relationship joys and struggles. The harsh realities of your day-to-day life confront your sweet fantasies of secure love as Venus—now sequestered in your 12th House of Inner Peace until **August 26**—opposes domineering Pluto on **August 1**. Your own emotions are raw; you might feel too vulnerable to engage in a confrontation about getting your needs met. Although your passions are aroused, you may choose to withdraw and save the battle for another day. You're more interested in building on what you've already created, and cerebral Mercury's entry into hardworking Virgo and your 2nd House of Personal Resources on **August 2** has you thinking about the practical side of things until it enters indulgent Libra on **August 25**.

The unsettling Aquarius Full Moon Eclipse on **August 5** can offer up a relationship surprise. You have one too many options with hyperactive Mars skating in Gemini through your 11th House of Goals, dispersing your focus. The push-pull theme becomes obvious if you compare the constraining forces of **August 10**—when hot Mars squares cold Saturn—with the potentially explosive energy of **August 18**, when he squares erratic Uranus. Suppressing your need for independence will not work, but be careful about overreacting or you'll upset the status quo. You may feel your resistance to change as you experience alternating waves of optimism and pessimism, culminating in an uncomfortable Jupiter-Saturn quincunx on **August 19**, followed by an expressive Leo New Moon on **August 20**.

SATURDAY 1	
SUNDAY 2	
MONDAY 3 ★	The current shift in dynamics is hopeful

TUESDAY 4 ★	
WEDNESDAY 5 ★ ○	
THURSDAY 6	
FRIDAY 7	
SATURDAY 8	
SUNDAY 9	
MONDAY 10 ★	**SUPER NOVA DAYS** Think before you act

TUESDAY 11 ★	
WEDNESDAY 12 ★	
THURSDAY 13 ★	
FRIDAY 14 ★	
SATURDAY 15 ★	
SUNDAY 16 ★	
MONDAY 17 ★	
TUESDAY 18	
WEDNESDAY 19	
THURSDAY 20 ★ ●	There are no simple answers to life's questions now

FRIDAY 21 ★	
SATURDAY 22 ★	
SUNDAY 23 ★	
MONDAY 24	
TUESDAY 25	
WEDNESDAY 26 ★	Be flexible enough to seek common ground

THURSDAY 27	
FRIDAY 28	
SATURDAY 29	
SUNDAY 30	
MONDAY 31	

★ designates key date

WHAT MATTERS MOST

Tensions at the beginning of the month can set the tone for relationship struggles; fortunately, you can learn a great deal about yourself and those around you in the process. Much of your time is spent reevaluating your recent interactions with others, sifting through the positive and the negative, and considering what changes you must make. Excessive Jupiter, emotionally wounded Chiron, and elusive Neptune, still traveling in a pack, are retrograde all month in your 7th House of Partnerships. Mercury's retrograde phase on **September 6-29** is a perfect opportunity to do this kind of relationship review and analysis, allowing you to be more discerning as it backs into organized Virgo in your 2nd House of Values on **September 17**.

A series of oppositions to the planets in your 7th House help you gain perspective on issues of the heart as loving Venus crosses Jupiter on **September 11**, Chiron on **September 14**, and Neptune on **September 15**. But the most significant aspect of the month is also on **September 15**, when reluctant Saturn opposes progressive Uranus in a series that began on **November 4, 2008**, and doesn't end until **July 26, 2010**. This wake-up call crosses your resource-oriented 2nd and 8th Houses, reminding you to pay close attention to what you own, what you earn, and what you want. You may feel a great sense of urgency to break out of the rut into which you have fallen, take immediate action to alleviate boredom, and multiply your resources. Keep in mind, however, that you're still in the middle of a long-term process. Don't expect amazing epiphanies to suddenly liberate you or a magical transporter beam to instantaneously take you to a galaxy far, far away.

TUESDAY 1 ★ Your actions are at odds with your thoughts now

WEDNESDAY 2 ★

THURSDAY 3 ★

FRIDAY 4 ★ ○

SATURDAY 5

SUNDAY 6

MONDAY 7

TUESDAY 8

WEDNESDAY 9

THURSDAY 10

FRIDAY 11 ★ Overindulge your senses in search of pleasure

SATURDAY 12 ★

SUNDAY 13

MONDAY 14

TUESDAY 15 ★ **SUPER NOVA DAYS** Don't wait to put a plan into action

---

WEDNESDAY 16 ★

THURSDAY 17 ★

FRIDAY 18 ★ ●

SATURDAY 19

SUNDAY 20 ★ Take time to enjoy yourself

MONDAY 21 ★

TUESDAY 22 ★

WEDNESDAY 23

THURSDAY 24

FRIDAY 25

SATURDAY 26

SUNDAY 27

MONDAY 28

TUESDAY 29

WEDNESDAY 30

ENDINGS AND BEGINNINGS

You are coming to the end of a circuitous journey that began in **September 2007**, when Saturn the Tester entered Virgo and your 2nd House of Self-Worth. Although this may have brought financial adversity, hopefully you were able to stabilize your material world and in the process clarify what is most important to you. If money is still tight, this month may prove to be a transition that lightens your worries. Saturn enters cooperative Libra and your 3rd House of Communication on **October 29**, a moment that can be a significant turning point as your hard work finally begins to pay off. This isn't an overnight success, but the first step in a process that will build momentum over the days and weeks ahead.

The fiery Aries Full Moon on **October 4** shows you the big picture and forces you to think about what you may be hiding. Assertive Mars's entry into demonstrative Leo on **October 16** enables you to take suppressed feelings and push them out into the open. Mars remains in exhibitionist Leo for the rest of the year as he slows down to turn retrograde on **December 20**. This extended visit by Mars gives you plenty of time to accomplish your goals, so rather than rushing in and doing sloppy work, take your time and get it right. Your imagination is vividly active, especially with respect to romance, when the lovely Libra New Moon on **October 18** aligns favorably with dreamy Neptune in your 7th House of Relationships. Remember that you are looking at others through a fantasy filter now, so be cautious about making commitments based upon your current experience.

THURSDAY 1	
FRIDAY 2	
SATURDAY 3	
SUNDAY 4 ★ ○ Keep impractical thoughts at bay	
MONDAY 5	
TUESDAY 6	
WEDNESDAY 7	
THURSDAY 8 ★ **SUPER NOVA DAYS** Denial won't work; discuss the problem	
FRIDAY 9 ★	
SATURDAY 10 ★	
SUNDAY 11	
MONDAY 12 ★ You are more organized than usual now	
TUESDAY 13 ★	
WEDNESDAY 14 ★	
THURSDAY 15 ★	
FRIDAY 16	
SATURDAY 17	
SUNDAY 18 ●	
MONDAY 19	
TUESDAY 20	
WEDNESDAY 21	
THURSDAY 22	
FRIDAY 23	
SATURDAY 24	
SUNDAY 25	
MONDAY 26	
TUESDAY 27	
WEDNESDAY 28 ★ Find a delicate path between two extremes	
THURSDAY 29 ★	
FRIDAY 30	
SATURDAY 31	

EXTREME MAKEOVER

You are beginning a long-term process by establishing healthy patterns in your everyday life that will sustain you for years to come. You can hear different footsteps coming down the planetary path now that Saturn the Taskmaster has entered your 3rd House of Immediate Environment. Personal success can be the result of working very hard to overcome limitations. Saturn forms a slow-moving square with Pluto the Terminator throughout this month, forcing you to eliminate destructive behavior and excessive consumption of resources. Although the square between persistent Saturn and transformative Pluto is exact on **November 15**, you will most likely feel the relentless pressure to change for the rest of the year.

The first few days of the month can be confusing as the sensual Taurus Full Moon pulls you back to your center while lovely Venus forms a relaxed trine with wistful Neptune on **November 2**, highlighting your world with the bright colors of your imagination. You believe that anything you want can be yours, only to face the challenge of putting your fantasies into language that others can understand. This metamorphosis does not come easily, and you may be quite unwilling to relinquish control; however, the powerful Saturn-Pluto square is unforgiving and will take from you whatever is necessary to make room for the positive changes ahead. Be smart by preemptively cutting waste, focusing your attention on what's most important, and voluntarily giving up your attachment to things that don't help your transformative process. If you're living a life aligned with your true purpose, this transit can guide you to the next level. But if you've lost your way, you may struggle now to regain your direction.

SUNDAY 1

MONDAY 2 ★ O Make use of your sharper communication skills

TUESDAY 3 ★

WEDNESDAY 4 ★

THURSDAY 5 ★

FRIDAY 6 ★ Stress and tension are increased in your daily routine

SATURDAY 7 ★

SUNDAY 8 ★

MONDAY 9

TUESDAY 10 ★ Painful memories are a challenge to face now

WEDNESDAY 11 ★

THURSDAY 12

FRIDAY 13

SATURDAY 14 ★ **SUPER NOVA DAYS** There are infinite possibilities everywhere you look

SUNDAY 15 ★

MONDAY 16 ★ ●

TUESDAY 17

WEDNESDAY 18

THURSDAY 19

FRIDAY 20

SATURDAY 21 ★ Set limits and stick to them

SUNDAY 22 ★

MONDAY 23 ★

TUESDAY 24 ★

WEDNESDAY 25 ★

THURSDAY 26 ★

FRIDAY 27

SATURDAY 28

SUNDAY 29

MONDAY 30

HOPING AND WISHING

If last month put you through the wringer, this one brings you out the other side. Not only can you see what may be around the next bend, but you also gain clarity about your recent challenges. You know that hard choices still need to be made, but understanding that these important decisions will take time can give you a reprieve for the holiday season. The third and final conjunction among boundless Jupiter, healing Chiron, and imaginative Neptune in your 7th House of Relationships can put an ethereal touch on the otherwise mundane activities of the month. The current gathering of these three spiritual planets can replay issues that were prominent in your life around **May 23–27** and **July 10–22**. Jupiter's conjunction with Chiron on **December 7** could offer hope and happiness—and although positive effects are likely, so is disappointment if your expectations are unrealistic. Jupiter's conjunction with Neptune on **December 21** is indicative of your current attraction to the subtle yet powerful experiences that transcend the three-dimensional world. Relationships, too, can seem infused with magic. Yet as glamorous as someone may appear, you must stay aware of where reality ends and your fantasies begin.

The playful Gemini Full Moon on **December 2** falls in your 11th House of Groups and Friends, raising the social bar and filling your calendar with fun yet distracting activities. The fun-loving Sagittarius New Moon on **December 16** falls in your 5th House of Love and Creativity, urging you to jump into the holiday spirit. You may choose to end the year on a retreat instead of going to a party, though, as the self-protective Cancer Full Moon Eclipse on **December 31** falls in your 12th House of Spirituality.

TUESDAY 1	
WEDNESDAY 2	○
THURSDAY 3	
FRIDAY 4	
SATURDAY 5	★ Perseverance is your smartest strategy

SUNDAY 6	★
MONDAY 7	★
TUESDAY 8	★
WEDNESDAY 9	★
THURSDAY 10	★
FRIDAY 11	
SATURDAY 12	
SUNDAY 13	
MONDAY 14	
TUESDAY 15	

WEDNESDAY 16 ★ ● **SUPER NOVA DAYS** Brush up your act before you take center stage

THURSDAY 17	★
FRIDAY 18	★
SATURDAY 19	★
SUNDAY 20	★

MONDAY 21 ★ Ponder the wonders of life

TUESDAY 22	
WEDNESDAY 23	

THURSDAY 24 ★ Introspection and contemplation fill the final days of the year

FRIDAY 25	★
SATURDAY 26	★
SUNDAY 27	
MONDAY 28	
TUESDAY 29	
WEDNESDAY 30	
THURSDAY 31	○

2010 HOROSCOPE

LEO

JULY 23–AUGUST 22

OVERVIEW OF THE YEAR

Unexpected twists and turns on the path of life alter your direction this year, Leo, while reminding you of the mysterious ways of fate. Unpredictable Uranus is now completing its extended stay—it arrived back in 2003—in emotional Pisces and your 8th House of Investments and Shared Resources. Your fiscal dependence on others—a business partner, a lover, even a bank—may have led you down a very different road from what you initially expected. Since the 8th House also symbolizes intimacy, you've probably experienced ups and downs as you attempted to manage the instability of those closest to you. **This year is transitional. Ready or not, you are required to taste of what lies ahead** when shocking Uranus explodes into impulsive Aries and your 9th House of Big Ideas on May 27. But on August 13, it retrogrades back into your hidden 8th House, granting you another six months as one last chance to complete old financial and emotional business.

Excitable Uranus is not alone, for exaggerated Jupiter enters your complex 8th House on

January 17, emphasizing the significance what lurks just beneath the surface. Optimistic Jupiter then enters fellow fire sign Aries on June 6 and conjoins Uranus on June 8 in the first of three eye-opening alignments that recur on September 18 and January 4, 2011. The initial conjunction is highly inspirational, falling in your 9th House of Future Vision. But the next two alignments are more immediate and personal—occurring in your intimate 8th House—indicating that **the great adventure on which you're ready to embark stems from your deepest passions**.

Meanwhile, taskmaster Saturn opposes the expansive Jupiter-Uranus conjunctions, preventing you from going overboard. As austere Saturn moves through graceful Libra and your 3rd House of Communication, you must spend your time wisely while restructuring the patterns of your everyday life. But Saturn slips back into your 2nd House of Money on April 7, giving you another opportunity to enhance your self-esteem and your finances before it reenters Libra on July 21. Saturn's recurring oppositions to Jupiter and Uranus throughout the year set up a theme of breaking through established boundaries. With

the financial and communication houses accentuated, you may see **material insecurities and even
losses turned into new confidence and gains,
reflecting your increased self-worth.**

Powerful Pluto stepped into your 6th House of
Self-Improvement in 2008 to begin a long-term
makeover of your health, habits, and daily routine.
You must make concrete changes as a hard square
from Saturn in your data-rich 3rd House feeds you
information that conflicts with what you already
know. **You may need to modify your lifestyle when
you realize that your current program isn't working as efficiently as you wish**. This transit began on
November 15, 2009, and repeats on January 31 and
August 21, suggesting that old worn-out excuses
won't serve your interests any longer.

PLAY IT AGAIN

Fiery Mars can heat up your love life as he visits heart-centered Leo until June 7, but since the warrior planet is retrograde until March 10, you could find yourself rekindling an old flame or rediscovering a scrapbook filled with pictures from a previous romance. You're driven to seek deeper meaning from relationships while bountiful Jupiter visits your 8th House of Intimacy from January 17 to June 6. Plant the seeds of your romantic dreams on February 13–16; take a risk on March 3; and reconsider your goals through the end of May. June brings a significant shift that brightens your heart and gets the adrenaline flowing. Still, there are challenges through the summer, especially July 29–August 11, when you will face important decisions. Venus's retrograde from October 8 to November 18 gives you a chance to revisit and resolve significant relationship issues that may have been previously too difficult to process.

A TWIST IN THE PLOT

Although you may need to prove yourself through extreme effort, your greatest reward this year will likely be a surprise. Strict Saturn frustrates you as it throws up obstacles that test your resolve. Its square to merciless Pluto—which began last November—requires you to overcome resistance on January 31 and August 21. You aren't being asked to play a minor role; you've been drafted as the star of your own professional drama. Opportunities tempt you on May 23 and August 16, yet you must demonstrate your worthiness before triumph can be yours. The tension is particularly high around April 26 and July 26, when stable Saturn's opposition to rebellious Uranus provokes you to overreact. Maintaining your cool and staying attentive to your long-term goals can set the stage for unexpected breakthroughs when prosperous Jupiter joins Uranus on June 8, September 18, and January 4, 2011.

LUCKY BREAK

You've recently had to take responsibility for your finances and, perhaps, deal with cash shortages as Saturn the Tester moved through your 2nd House of Possessions from September 2, 2007, through October 29, 2008. This year, frugal Saturn retrogrades back into your 2nd House on April 7, forcing you to reevaluate your previous successes and failures and make necessary fiscal changes by July 21, when it leaves your money house. Fortunately, you receive help from other individuals, investors, or a financial institution when beneficent Jupiter visits your 8th House of Shared Resources from January 17 to June 6 and then again on September 9 to January 22, 2011.

NO TIME LIKE THE PRESENT

The New Moon Eclipse in ambitious Capricorn on January 15 falls in your 6th House of Health, signaling the need for change. Get a complete physical, even if you feel healthy: It's always best to be fully informed. If you're willing to do the work, you'll see positive results from changes in your lifestyle. But this is no time to be lazy. Eclipses are notorious for bringing issues into awareness, especially those you're trying to avoid. The Capricorn Full Moon Eclipse on June 26 joins regenerative Pluto, reminding you that there's no time to waste. But don't take any shortcuts. No fad diets or quick cures for you now; the changes must become an integral part of your life. Pluto is particularly stressed during the summer, so don't wait to make the necessary improvements.

RESOURCE MANAGEMENT

Your biggest challenge this year will be handling
growth. Forces are conspiring to lure you out into
the world—and as your horizons expand, pressure
rises in your home and family life. Instead of view-
ing this as a battleground, try to enroll others to
work with you; convincing them that your success
is their success could help everyone feel more
connected. Finally, you may get some well-
deserved downtime—or might be required to work
at home—when Venus enters your 4th House of
Domestic Conditions on September 8, followed
by Mars on September 14. The next couple of
months can be a great time to start a renovation
project or to complete an unfinished one,
especially when Venus is retrograde October 8–
November 18.

SPROUTING WINGS

Your mind hits the road this year. It may be very difficult to contain your wanderlust when surprising Uranus bolts into go-getter Aries and your 9th House of Adventure on May 27, staying there until August 13. Globetrotting Jupiter joins the fun June 6–September 9, opening the travel window of opportunity even wider. Still, getting away may be trickier than you imagine. Serious Saturn rests in your 3rd House of Short Trips for most of the year, demanding that you stay closer to home to fulfill domestic and professional responsibilities. If possible, wait until after July 21 to go on the adventure of a lifetime.

WAKE-UP CALL

The recurring conjunction of Uranus the Awakener and visionary Jupiter is like a meta-physical alarm clock that goes off in your 9th House of Big Ideas on June 8, echoing through your life and resonating with you through the rest of the year. Deepen your commitment to your spiritual path or make time to pursue a new course of personal development. The receptive Cancer New Moon Eclipse on July 11 falls in your 12th House of Spirituality, activating warning lights in your dreams if you aren't paying attention to your inner path.

RICK & JEFF'S TIP FOR THE YEAR
Ask for Help

You expect great things from yourself, Leo, and
you can work quite hard once you make a sincere
commitment. This is why you must now think
carefully about any promises you make—to yourself or anyone else. There are powerful forces at
play that can lure you into believing that anything
is possible. It's true that this year brings great
potential, but exhausting yourself trying to
achieve the impossible dream is not a sensible
strategy. Heed the counsel of wise friends and
seasoned professionals before making any
life-changing decisions.

JANUARY

READY, AIM, DON'T FIRE

Powerful forces restrain your creative self-expression this month. Constrictive Saturn is moving toward an exact square with relentless Pluto on **January 31**, reemphasizing work-related problems that first surfaced last fall. Still, you're burning brighter than usual with fiery Mars in your sign until **June 7**. Normally the action planet heats up each sign for about two months, but this time you have the mixed blessing of Mars in lively Leo for nearly eight. You were first blasted with a round of excitement when Mars entered Leo and your 1st House of Self on **October 16, 2009**, but may have run into trouble expressing your exuberance. Energetic Mars turned retrograde on **December 20, 2009**, to put on your brakes. He remains retrograde until **March 10**, leaving you frustrated—but probably not enough dampen your enthusiasm. Instead of wasting your time wondering why you aren't making more progress, use this time to build your strength for a more determined forward march in a couple of months.

It's doubly hard to manage the excess energy that Mars brings into your life now because communicator planet Mercury, too, is retrograde. You'll get a glimpse of the future, though, when the messenger planet finally turns direct on **January 15**, the same day as the New Moon Eclipse in ambitious Capricorn. Managing your anger can be crucial to your happiness right now. Yes, information is beginning to flow more easily, but you cannot escape the continued backward pull of Mars yet. Be careful about inadvertently turning a minor disagreement into a major one on **January 30**, when the Leo Full Moon is conjunct combative Mars.

KEEP IN MIND THIS MONTH

A setback is not the same thing as a failure.
Keep your eyes on the prize, even
if it's still a few months away.

KEY DATES

★ **JANUARY 1–5**
make love, not war

You're raring to go, but potent forces slow you.
Multiple magical quintiles affecting your 6th
House of Health and Work show you brilliant
new solutions to old familiar problems. Still, a
tense connection between macho Mars and
dominating Pluto on **January 3** can find you
itching for a fight. Don't spend so much time
keeping score and planning your revenge that
you miss the beauty right in front of your nose
on **January 5** when mischievous Mercury
quickly kisses lovely Venus.

★ **JANUARY 13–15**
no sleeping on the job

Pay close attention to your daily routine now,
for the New Moon Solar Eclipse in pragmatic
Capricorn on **January 15** can bring an
unpleasant surprise if you don't manage
details carefully. Luckily, beautiful Venus
joins the eclipse in your 6th House of Self-
Improvement, and with supportive sextiles to

Uranus the Awakener on **January 13**, increased awareness is the most important thing you can add to the equation. Don't miss this opportunity to make changes that will have a positive impact on your well-being.

★ **JANUARY 17–19**
room at the top
You see far into your future during these transitional days. Deep emotional changes clear away obstacles to reveal a whole new landscape as visionary Jupiter enters imaginative Pisces on **January 17**. Then, on **January 18–19** when Venus and the Sun enter intelligent Aquarius and your 7th House of Partners, others can help you reevaluate your assumptions about relationships, giving you clarity on commitment issues that once held you back.

★ **JANUARY 22–24**
consider the long-term benefits
Calm waters may encourage you to relax, yet this is no time to fall asleep at the wheel.

Formalizing a partnership is a wise move with lasting value on **January 22**, when rich Venus in your 7th House of Companions trines stabilizing Saturn. The Sun joins the trine on **January 24**, confirming your sound judgment. Make something happen, even if it's just planning an event for the future.

SUPER NOVA DAYS

★ **JANUARY 27–31**
stormy weather

Retrograde Mars stirs up relationship stress when he opposes romantic Venus on **January 27**. Then an intense Mars-Pluto connection on **January 28** gives you transformative psychological tools to work with as your anger pushes up against current circumstances. The proud Leo Full Moon on **January 30** exposes your suppressed emotions and brings your true intentions out into the open. With warrior Mars nearby, conflicts are possible, even if the situation doesn't warrant a fight. Saturn's square to Pluto on **January 31** is a reminder that working with these powerful feelings is a long-term process.

FEBRUARY

TIME TO HEAL

You spend much of this month trying to establish a new direction, but you may not make much progress until you accept the role you play in the lives of those around you. Energetic Mars continues his retrograde phase in your 1st House of Self, challenging you to maintain your normally healthy sense of identity. Meanwhile, relationships demand that you change your perspective and look at yourself more objectively. Yet this is tricky, for far-reaching Jupiter—now moving through your 8th House of Deep Sharing—is first uncomfortably restrained by unyielding Saturn and then intensified by passionate Pluto on **February 5–6**, giving you new insight into what others are feeling.

The progressive Aquarius New Moon on **February 13** is conjunct sympathetic Chiron and spiritual Neptune. It falls in your 7th House of Partnerships, planting seeds for connections that contain the dreams of your future. The Chiron-Neptune conjunction is exact on **February 17**, suggesting that real healing begins in your imagination. Chiron activates memories of old wounds, yet compassionate Neptune teaches you how to forgive

65

others and yourself, allowing you to move past the pain associated with these hurtful experiences. The focus is on others because a minimum of four planets remain in your 7th House until the Sun heads into the emotional waters of Pisces on **February 18**. As your feelings intensify through the latter part of the month, the analytical Virgo Full Moon on **February 28** falls in your 2nd House of Self-Worth. This returns your focus to the practical details of handling your finances and managing yourself and your resources more carefully.

KEEP IN MIND THIS MONTH

Grueling as it is to be vulnerable, a heartfelt apology for a previous misdeed is far better than avoiding the issue entirely.

KEY DATES

★ **FEBRUARY 5–6**
proceed with caution
Prepare for confusion on **February 5**, when optimistic Jupiter forms an uneasy quincunx to pessimistic Saturn. It's part of a long-term pattern that began last year, challenging you with contradictory strategies for getting ahead. With Jupiter in your 8th House of Investments and Shared Resources, you may be ready, even eager, to pursue an opportunity with a generous partner, yet circumstances or your own fears prevent you from jumping in too quickly. Luckily, Jupiter's supportive sextile with relentless Pluto on **February 6** indicates eventual success as long as you work not just yourself, but for the benefit of all involved.

SUPER NOVA DAYS

★ **FEBRUARY 10–13**
all things considered
Everything you fix seems to create a new problem as assertive Mars forms annoying quincunxes with overblown Jupiter and obsessive

Pluto on **February 10–12**. Your just-do-it attitude can backfire, even if you have the best of intentions. Just when you're pushed to the edge and ready to give up, logical Mercury and lovable Venus enter new signs, changing the landscape of your interactions with others. Even if you're unsure what you want, you sound more certain as you talk about your goals, especially when Mercury gets an authoritative nod of approval from Saturn on **February 12**. Your likelihood for successful communication continues to increase through the intelligent Aquarius New Moon on **February 13**. Although this can be a positive turning point in a relationship, be careful not to start an unnecessary fight by insisting you have all the answers.

★ **FEBRUARY 15–16**
lost and found
You receive mixed messages from someone close to you. Although sweet Venus sextiles shadowy Pluto on **February 15** to intensify your feelings, the rewards can be significant if you delve deeply into the unknown when Venus meets opportunistic Jupiter on **February 16**. But

Mars in expressive Leo connects with hardworking Saturn, so don't be passive and wait for something wonderful to happen. Apply what you know in a practical manner. There's no need to doubt yourself; you're on the right track.

★ **FEBRUARY 27–28**
the devil is in the details
Let go of your need to rationalize your ideas when Mercury the Communicator joins Neptune the Dissolver on **February 27**. Although fantasy offers a different view of the truth—a symbolic way to see your world— the practical Virgo Full Moon shows you reality in its true light. Still, it's challenging to pay attention to all the details when the Full Moon opposes an overwhelming Sun-Jupiter conjunction on **February 28**.

MARCH

RED LIGHT, GREEN LIGHT

Hold on to your hat, Leo, because the winds of change are blowing in your direction . . . and you're going to like where they take you. Feisty Mars in playful Leo turned retrograde in your 1st House of Self on **December 20, 2009**, inhibiting your self-expression and slowing your forward progress. This frustrating period ends when Mars turns direct on **March 10**, beginning a party that lasts until he leaves your sign on **June 7**. There are other indications that your waiting period is finally over. You get an early go-ahead on **March 7** when friendly Venus enters enthusiastic Aries and harmoniously trines Mars, signaling a spring thaw in your love life. Talkative Mercury makes the same transition into Aries and your 9th House of Big Ideas on **March 17**. The truth seems clear now, so communicate your position with unwavering confidence. Finally, the Sun enters Aries on **March 20**. This is the Spring Equinox, a time of creation and initiation for all. But for you, its special meaning is tied to the Sun's easy trine to Mars on **March 21**. Suddenly you have the stamina to accomplish more than you expect.

It's not all easy going, of course. You may need to overcome resistance when Venus, Mercury, and the Sun oppose restrictive Saturn in social Libra on **March 9**, **March 18, and March 21**, respectively. Several planets linger in your 8th House of Transformation for much of the month, yet change comes slowly. The magical Pisces New Moon falls in your emotional 8th House on **March 15**, inspiring you to plant seeds of intention from which intimacy can grow. The relationship-oriented Libra Full Moon on **March 29** encourages you to confront your personal needs while also respecting those of close friends and partners.

KEEP IN MIND THIS MONTH

Spring fever puts a twinkle in your eyes and warms the fire in your heart, but don't expect miracles. It takes time for momentum to build.

KEY DATES

★ **MARCH 1–3**
surprise ending
Mercury's irritating quincunxes from the 8th
House of Intimacy to pushy Mars on **March 1**
and prudent Saturn on **March 2** may have you
rushing into a deep emotional conversation
one minute and planning your escape route
the next. But you're likely to throw caution to
the wind when delicious Venus meets up with
unorthodox Uranus on **March 3**. Take a risk
and plunge into the unknown, but know that
events probably won't turn out as you planned.

★ **MARCH 7–9**
fire and ice
Romantic Venus starts a new cycle by stepping
into courageous Aries on **March 7**, kicking up
the chemistry while a sexy Venus-Mars trine
heats your feelings even more. Go ahead and
ask for your heart's desire when chatty
Mercury joins confident Jupiter as you're
extremely persuasive now in business and in
love. But the flames flicker when Venus

opposes sobering Saturn on **March 9**. This reality check can change your perspective; getting everything you want now is not as important as behaving responsibly.

SUPER NOVA DAYS

★ **MARCH 15–18**
rude awakening

Lightning strikes—and transports you to a new dimension—when the psychic Pisces New Moon joins cerebral Mercury and shocking Uranus on **March 15**. This marks the end of an emotional cycle that can suddenly turn your life around. Mercury enters pioneering Aries on **March 17** and trines aggressive Mars to add force to your words. However, if you favor conflict over conversation, Mercury's tense opposition with stern Saturn on **March 18** will put an immediate stop to your wicked ways. The brilliant ideas and clever words that brought you here can't help you now. Get real, respect authority, and adjust your thinking as required.

★ **MARCH 21–22**
heroic effort
What looks like smooth sailing on **March 21**
when the Sun harmonizes with Mars quickly
turns choppy as the Sun forms its yearly opposition with parental Saturn. Yes morphs into no
right before your eyes. But don't give up: An
industrious Mars-Saturn sextile on **March 22**
enables you to snatch victory from the jaws
of defeat.

★ **MARCH 25**
smart offense
A new kind of resistance surfaces today and
it's not just a simple roadblock. You face a formidable—and resourceful—opponent at work
as the Sun squares vengeful Pluto. Instead of
engaging directly, create a strategy that allows
you to defuse the conflict while also demonstrating your ability to handle complexity. Turn
this battle for survival into a win–win situation.

APRIL

MAKE IT REAL

Your life is on the move now that outgoing Mars in bighearted Leo has resumed direct motion, but great ideas and good intentions are not enough to guarantee success. You need common sense, too—and it may call for scaling back your plans. Mercury enters back-to-basics Taurus on **April 2**, downshifting your speedy mental processes to a slower, more methodical pace. Sometimes Mercury can run through a house in two weeks, but this time it turns retrograde on **April 18**, then hangs around in your 10th House of Career until **June 10**. Focus on your success in the public eye—yet use the time when the communication planet is backing through familiar territory to review your professional goals and rethink current strategies.

On **April 7**, karmic Saturn retrogrades back into exacting Virgo and your 2nd House of Money, another indicator that you can't forge ahead until your material ducks are in a row. The irrepress-ible Aries New Moon in your 9th House of Future Vision on **April 14** tempts you to force a change that aligns your life with your dreams. But the

Sun's entry into Taurus on **April 20** is just one more sign that mundane matters are temporarily more important than the most alluring fantasy. This tension between your previous commitments and your need for something wildly different increases throughout the month until something suddenly gives. A slow-moving opposition between responsible Saturn and radical Uranus is exact on **April 26**, suggesting that you can't contain yourself any longer. The resourceful Scorpio Full Moon on **April 28** is opposite generous Venus and the Sun in your public 10th House. Recognition and success can be yours . . . if you are really want them.

KEEP IN MIND THIS MONTH

Don't think you're doing something wrong just because your dreams are slow to manifest. Stay grounded, and your persistence will be rewarded.

KEY DATES

★ **APRIL 1**
sleight of mind
Magic is in the air, and it's not a slick disap-
pearing card trick; this is something deeper
and much more entrancing. Omnipotent
Jupiter in your 8th House of Regeneration
quintiles potent Pluto in your 6th House of
Work to unleash the power of change. Right
now, the strength of your convictions is
enough to bring transformation. There's
no need to wave a wizardly wand; just move
your mind.

★ **APRIL 3–6**
hooked on a feeling
Venus and Mars lock horns in a spicy square
on **April 3** that stirs uneasy romantic attractions. Luckily, sensual Venus moves on to harmoniously trine passionate Pluto on **April 4**,
adding substance to your feelings and intimacy
to your interactions. When communicator
Mercury in your 10th House of Status squares
contentious Mars on **April 5**, you incorrectly

think you must defend your honor. Tempers
flare, but Mercury's trine to Pluto on **April 6**
allows you to bring the conversation back to
real issues. Discussing what motivated the
conflict is your key to resolving it.

★ **APRIL 10**
truth and consequences
You struggle to be true to yourself without
angering others during today's uneasy quincunx between expressive Mars and repressive
Pluto. Holding back the wave of feelings is
futile, yet the situation escalates once you
start to show your true colors. Staying aware
of how others may react to your emotions can
help you frame them more constructively.

★ **APRIL 17–19**
dangling conversations
You see the silver lining in every dark cloud on
April 17 thanks to a beautiful Venus-Jupiter
alignment. The Sun's sweet sextile with imaginative Neptune the next day makes the good
news even better as your fantasies kick in. But
a communication hang-up can flip your world

upside down when Mercury turns retrograde, too. Don't expect a quick fix: A quirky quincunx between the Sun and taciturn Saturn on **April 19** points you toward additional discussions.

SUPER NOVA DAYS

★ **APRIL 23-26**
apocalypse not now
Everything in your life is stretched to the max during the days preceding the strained Saturn-Uranus opposition on **April 26**. Your dreams lure you into Fantasyland when enticing Venus squares foggy Neptune on **April 23**. First you're willing to wait for satisfaction; then you grow restless. By **April 25**, when retrograde Mercury squares militant Mars, your impatience can prod you right into verbal warfare. But the last Saturn-Uranus opposition in the series occurs on **July 26**, so you have more time before you must give the universe your final answer.

MAY

WAITING IN THE WINGS

Although you may be lost in confusion as the month begins, clarity rolls in like well-formed waves to give new purpose to your life. A tricky quincunx between realistic Saturn in your 2nd House of Self-Worth and hazy Neptune on **May 2** has you wondering if you're misleading yourself. Having the courage to question your core values is healthy, but don't be surprised if the malaise grows as you dig deeper. Though your bout with uncertainty may not be resolved until the Saturn-Neptune alignment repeats on **June 27**, a lot can change before then. Luckily, Mercury's retrograde period ends on **May 11**, freeing you from your protracted rehash of recent career decisions. Additionally, when the practical Taurus New Moon on **May 13** falls in your 10th House of Status, you must pull back from your esoteric search for truth in order to take on more responsibility at work.

Even if you're determined to fulfill past obligations, doing so becomes more challenging when enthusiastic Jupiter in your 8th House of Shared Resources moves to oppose hardworking Saturn on **May 23**—the first of three such alignments that recur on **August 16** and **March 28, 2011**. You intuitively know that current opportunities can lead to big rewards—emotionally and financially—yet you aren't able to say yes until you've tied up old business. Don't overreact by closing down and being overly cautious; however, carelessness is potentially just as dangerous. Patience and perseverance are wise options whenever you're in doubt. Nevertheless, your restlessness is tricky to contain when the adventurous Sagittarius Full Moon falls in your 5th House of Spontaneity on **May 27**, the same day unruly Uranus enters rowdy Aries and your 9th House of Future Vision.

KEEP IN MIND THIS MONTH

Don't be hard on yourself if you can't commit to long-range plans. A great transition lies before you, making it impossible to see around the bend.

KEY DATES

★ **MAY 2–4**
unstable conditions
You may find it hard to uncover the source
of your low spirits as the anxious Saturn-
Neptune alignment on **May 2** casts a pensive
mood over your life. Mover Mars runs into
somber Saturn on **May 3**, and your actions just
don't have the impact you hoped for. Your
frustration increases when logical Mercury
aspects passionate Pluto, making you less
willing to compromise. Managing your anger
is crucial when the Sun, Mars, and unreliable
Uranus stressfully align on **May 4**, possibly
provoking unproductive conflict. It's up to
you to express your feelings without
emotional drama.

★ **MAY 10–13**
no quick solution
The Sun in your 10th House of Career tensely
hooks up with domineering Pluto in your 6th
House of Employment on **May 10**, forcing you
to handle an unpleasant power struggle that's

brewing at work. You may feel hopeless when you realize how little leverage you have in the situation. Still, erupting won't bring satisfaction; simmer down until Mercury turns direct on **May 11**. It may take a few more days for your action plan to gel, too, so wait until after the New Moon in your public 10th House on **May 13** to make your move.

SUPER NOVA DAYS

★ **MAY 17–20**

there will be an answer; let it be

If you're holding on to unresolved grievances, your annoyance dissipates on **May 17** as the Sun and loving Venus align with abundant Jupiter in your 8th House of Shared Resources. But finances might turn problematic the next day, when Venus runs into austere Saturn in your 2nd House of Money. You may waver between confidently believing that anything is possible and then doubting yourself, sure that nothing of any consequence will happen. A breakthrough occurs on **May 19** when Venus squares electric Uranus, surprising you with an unexpected answer. Your shock turns to acceptance on **May 20** as the Sun enters adaptable Gemini in your 11th House of Long-Term Goals.

★ **MAY 27**
the times they are a-changin'
An inspirational Sagittarius Full Moon reminds you that something off the charts is about to happen. You are standing on the edge of a very exciting time in your life today as astonishing Uranus leaves emotionally sensitive Pisces—where it's been since 2003—and enters self-willed Aries. This long-term visit to your 9th House of Travel and Higher Education will likely change everything. Your horizons widen to bring faraway places close, and your mind opens to attract unfamiliar philosophies and ideas. Get ready for an amazing ride.

JUNE

READY TO ROCK AND ROLL

Fasten your seat belt, for this month takes off quickly and the surprises keep on coming. Perhaps you recently broke free from some aspect of your past, but when boundless Jupiter enters just-do-it Aries on **June 6** and joins unorthodox Uranus on **June 8**, the potential for change dramatically increases. This once-every-thirteen-year alignment occurs in your 9th House of Higher Education and Long Journeys, so push back the walls of limitations and open your mind to what lies ahead. Opportunities for travel could suddenly appear, yet it's a smart idea to combine a recreational trip with a learning experience. Think about beginning a course of study that puts you in touch with ideas from other times and distant places. As obstacles drop away—allowing you to see the big picture—you must quickly prioritize your choices or you could be so over-whelmed that you do nothing at all. Fortunately, insistent Mars—which has pumped up your sign since **October 16, 2009**—enters analytical Virgo on **June 7**, enabling you to narrow your focus and concentrate your physical energy.

You may have trouble making up your mind on **June 12** thanks to a New Moon in dualistic Gemini. Don't be disconcerted; the future is nearer than you think This lunation activates your 11th House of Dreams and Wishes, indicating that what you choose today will surely impact your long-term goals. Tension between the past and the future resurfaces when the Sun squares karmic Saturn, unstable Uranus, and opinionated Jupiter on **June 19–23**, forcing you to rectify a stressful situation. Small yet definitive steps are necessary when the goal-oriented Capricorn Full Moon Eclipse on **June 26** conjuncts transformative Pluto in your 6th House of Self-Improvement.

KEEP IN MIND THIS MONTH

You have been waiting a long time for the opportunities that are now available. Be courageous and step willingly into your future.

KEY DATES

★ **JUNE 1–2**
aim for the stars
You have a chance to radically change your life.
Don't be afraid to take it. Still, opening your
heart to surprise may take a conscious effort
when the Sun forms magical quintiles with
lucky Jupiter on **June 1** and with Uranus on
June 2. Use your common sense to bring these
possibilities down to a manageable level, for
attractive Venus quintiles concrete Saturn,
enabling you to manifest what you imagine.

SUPER NOVA DAYS

★ **JUNE 4–8**
brave new world
You sense the calm before the storm when
action-planet Mars opposes diffusive Neptune
on **June 4**. But confident Jupiter's shift into
enterprising Aries and its alignment with
explosive Uranus on **June 6–8** blast you into
the future. This can be thrilling yet destabiliz-
ing and it's hard to keep your balance, even as
Mars enters earthy Virgo on **June 7**. Don't get

sidetracked by the immediate effects of your behavior. Just keep making the necessary adjustments until Mercury's harmonizing trine to steady Saturn on **June 8** sets your feet back on solid ground.

★ **JUNE 10–12**
don't sweat the small stuff
Your thoughts can distract you during the days leading up to the restless Gemini New Moon on **June 12**. Quicksilver Mercury returns home to Gemini on **June 10**, increasing your mental chatter. Its tense square from your 11th House of Friends to aggressive Mars on **June 11** can provoke angry words over trivial matters. Fortunately, the unsettled energies are soothed by a coolheaded Venus-Saturn sextile. Simpler times lie ahead.

★ **JUNE 19–23**
rainbow in the sky
The Summer Solstice on **June 21** is usually a time of respite when the Sun enters protective Cancer and your reclusive 12th House. Don't expect much rest this year, however, for you

must make some significant decisions about
your life's direction. The Sun's square to
somber Saturn on **June 19** is cause for self-
doubt, yet its square to brilliant Uranus creates flashes of awareness on **June 21**. Just
be sure not to overreact—an extravagant
Sun-Jupiter square on **June 23** encourages
exaggeration.

★ **JUNE 25–26**
high voltage, low threshold
Hold on a few more days, Leo: Things will
settle down soon. You're already riding a roller
coaster on **June 25** as an electric Mercury-
Uranus square sends sparks of lightning
through your nervous system and a powerful
Sun-Pluto opposition dares you to fight to
the finish. The instability grows through the
Capricorn Full Moon Eclipse on **June 26**, which
can clear the air of hidden hostilities and
make for smoother sailing ahead.

JULY

SHINE ON

Don't procrastinate—there's no time to waste with the Sun and Mercury lingering in your 12th House of Endings at the beginning of the month. Have your story ready to tell on **July 9** when chatty Mercury enters showy Leo, where it remains until **July 29**. Meanwhile, stylish Venus in Leo continues to bless you with sparkling charm and growing popularity. You can develop a better relationship with money, your possessions, and even your self-esteem when Venus moves into your 2nd House of Self-Worth on **July 10**. The New Moon Eclipse in moody Cancer on **July 11** falls in your private 12th House, indicating that you may be keeping your plans to yourself until they are ready to hatch.

On **July 21**, strategic Saturn returns to creative-thinking Libra and your 3rd House of Communication, where it previously visited from **October 29, 2009**, through **April 7**. Reconsider ways to improve the efficiency of your interactions with others on both a business and a personal level. You take center stage as the Sun enters your sign on **July 22**, but be careful of overconfidence when pompous Jupiter squares powerful Pluto on

July 25, the same day that the Full Moon in eccentric Aquarius falls in your 7th House of Partners. Leaving a little room for self-doubt and humility can make you more accessible to others and increase your chances for success. Meanwhile, the pressure of Saturn's final opposition to surprising Uranus on **July 26** activates your communication houses. You'll dazzle everyone with your brilliance, as long as you don't wait until the last minute to prepare.

KEEP IN MIND THIS MONTH

Working diligently will serve you better than putting things off. Advance preparation will release pent-up tensions instead of driving them deeper within.

KEY DATES

★ **JULY 1–3**
like a prayer
Sharing a dream can be the clearest way to
express what you want when assertive Mars
and intuitive Neptune hook up with talkative
Mercury in your 12th House of Fantasy on **July 1**.
Luckily, Mercury receives help from solid
Saturn on **July 3**, enabling you to reinforce
your ideas with skillfully presented facts.

★ **JULY 8–11**
waiting is the hardest part
You find your goals mixed up with your
illusions when soft Venus opposes fantasy-
prone Neptune on **July 8**. You're seeing
others through Technicolor glasses now,
so don't make any long-term relationship
or financial decisions yet. Wait until logical
Mercury enters your sign and trines bright
Uranus on **July 9**; sparks will light up your
brain to reveal the truth. Then wait a bit
longer until the Cancer Solar Eclipse on
July 11 aligns with forceful Mars, empowering

your emotions and giving you the ability to
act decisively on your feelings.

★ **JULY 13**
searching for a four-leaf clover
A showy Leo Moon encourages you to play your
hand out in the open, while an intense Venus-
Pluto connection adds undeniable passion to
everything you touch. Valuable Venus, now in
efficient Virgo and your 2nd House of Resources,
offers the prospect of financial success.
However, her annoying quincunx to opulent
Jupiter indicates that you could overestimate
the reward . . . only to end up disappointed and
discouraged. Wealth could be elusive.

★ **JULY 22–23**
reversal of fortune
Your energy level goes up a notch when the Sun
begins its annual visit to your sign on **July 22**.
Fortunately, a supportive sextile to persistent
Saturn suggests that sound judgment and
hard work will ensure good results from your
current efforts to improve your life. The Sun's
superconductive trine to unpredictable Uranus

on **July 23** can suddenly shift the energy, bringing you quite a surprise. There's no need to resist the changes; once the shock has worn off, you'll quickly see the positive potential in the new situation.

SUPER NOVA DAYS

★ **JULY 25–26**
rebel without a clue
As the culmination of a series of events that began around **November 4, 2008**, Saturn the Taskmaster completes its tug-of-war with Uranus the Awakener on **July 26**. This opposition activates your 3rd House of Communication and your 9th House of Big Ideas, cranking up the tension if someone in control resists your plans. A powerful Jupiter-Pluto square, combined with the quirky Aquarius Full Moon on **July 25**, encourages you to take an unnecessary risk. Caution is a better choice; you have invested too much to jeopardize your future now.

AUGUST

NO PAIN, NO GAIN

Your daily routines undergo significant stress this month, so it's crucial to maintain a healthy diet and exercise program while also getting plenty of rest. Regenerative Pluto is making a long-term visit to your 6th House of Self-Improvement, but old habits must die before new ones are born. Optimistic Jupiter in your 9th House of Big Ideas squares Pluto on **August 3**. Your confidence is overinflated, and you may need to restrain your ambitions, especially if you've recently taken on too much work. It's time to pay the piper on **August 16**, when expansive Jupiter's opposition to restrictive Saturn reveals where you've overextended yourself or made promises you can't keep.

A cycle is completed on **August 21**, when Saturn in your 3rd House of Communication squares Pluto. The limitations you began to confront at the previous occurrences of this dynamic transit— on **November 15, 2009**, and **January 31**—now challenge you to overcome whatever still stands in your way. Unfortunately, brute force won't work. You could exhaust yourself winning every battle while still losing the war. Instead, decide what you can eliminate now to ensure your overall success.

The ego-driven Leo New Moon on **August 9** reveals the differences between who you are and how you want to be seen. Don't judge yourself harshly; just improve yourself however you can. On **August 20**, Mercury begins its retrograde phase in your 2nd House of Self-Worth, turning your thoughts inward as you question your worth and reconsider your financial choices. The empathic Pisces Full Moon on **August 24** falls in your 8th House of Deep Sharing, encouraging you to involve others in your ongoing process of transformation.

KEEP IN MIND THIS MONTH

Stressful situations remind you to handle the issues you've previously dodged. Expecting too much change, too fast is unrealistic; look to small adjustments.

KEY DATES

★ **AUGUST 3–4**
force of nature
You're challenged to maintain a realistic
perspective on **August 3**, when lavish Jupiter
and impassioned Pluto cross paths, as they
did on **July 25**, emboldening you to pursue your
goals without considering the needs of others.
An additional boost of energy arrives as auda-
cious Mars drives you even harder on **August 4**.
If you're unaware of your impact on others, you
may be puzzled when they lash back. Moderate
your intensity to solve problems before they occur.

★ **AUGUST 7–10**
instant karma
Although personable Venus is at home in
graceful Libra, she isn't very agreeable now
when aligning with wacky Uranus, solemn
Saturn, bombastic Jupiter, and ruthless Pluto.
You might be convinced that indulging yourself
will bring happiness, only to discover that satisfaction is elusive. You could become obsessive
on the days prior to the Leo New Moon on

August 9. Extreme behavior precipitates intense emotional reactions when sensual Venus squares Pluto on **August 10**. You can't escape the consequences of your actions if you think you're entitled to something you are not.

★ AUGUST 13–16
knowing versus doing
Lightning-like Uranus retrogrades back into sympathetic Pisces and your 8th House of Intimacy on **August 13** to give you a remedial course in learning to share with others. This transit lasts until **March 11, 2011**, but emotional breakthroughs in relationships could start right away. However, it may take a while to integrate your new perspective and to communicate it to others, because cautious Saturn in your 3rd House of Information opposes joyful Jupiter on **August 16**.

SUPER NOVA DAYS

★ AUGUST 20–21
inevitable truth
Expect confusion when the Sun opposes cloudy Neptune of **August 20**, the same day trickster Mercury turns retrograde. You're sent

back to the drawing board to reevaluate all
your plans, and this isn't just a casual intellectual exercise. Stern Saturn's square to insistent Pluto on **August 21** forces you to negotiate
when your instinct is to stubbornly dig in your
heels. It's your choice; rigid determination
could leave you cold and isolated, while flexi-
bility allows you to move through irrevocable
change with uncommon grace.

★ **AUGUST 24-26**
time to go
The Pisces Full Moon on **August 24** is a turning point for you—and the culmination of a
month of intense pressure to change the ways
you communicate with others. Although you
will continue to process recent events, the
Sun's anxious quincunx to far-reaching Jupiter
requires you to look ahead, even if that makes
you uncomfortable. Fortunately, the Sun's
harmonious trine to transformative Pluto on
August 26 helps you let go of the past and
bravely move on.

SEPTEMBER

REWRITING HISTORY

It's time to rethink your basic assumptions about finances when mental Mercury in analytical Virgo retrogrades through your 2nd House of Money and Resources to start your month. The Virgo New Moon on **September 8** reemphasizes your material 2nd House, focusing your attention on things rather than ideas. Although Mercury turns direct on **September 12**, encouraging you to think more about the future than the past, it will still be traveling over familiar ground for most of the month, blocking your view of the road ahead. Also, you experience an overall shift toward deepening your connection with the past as Venus, Jupiter, and Mars each enter emotional water signs. Alluring Venus enters inquisitive Scorpio and your 4th House of Roots on **September 8**, followed by energetic Mars on **September 14**. This spicy planetary pair travels together throughout the month, stimulating memories of childhood, home, and family. Share these with a loved one to sweeten intimacy.

Your nostalgia is accentuated when retrograde Jupiter backs into otherworldly Pisces and your

8th House of Deep Sharing on **September 9**. Visionary Jupiter joins out-of-the-blue Uranus on **September 18**, suddenly revealing long-forgotten episodes from your past that can help you tell your personal story in a different way. You may feel quite certain that something big is about to change—only to see your life settle down again after the Sun opposes Jupiter and Uranus on **September 21**. The Sun slips into harmonious Libra on **September 22**, marking the Fall Equinox. This is a time to seek balance, even if everything still feels somewhat chaotic. But complications at work and home won't likely be simplified until after **September 23**, when the irrepressible Aries Full Moon enables you to reveal your new personal vision for what's ahead.

KEEP IN MIND THIS MONTH

Reminiscing about hard times or the good old days helps you reprocess your personal history and face the future with wisdom and a fresh perspective.

KEY DATES

★ **SEPTEMBER 3–4**
words get in the way
It's hard to tell anyone exactly what you think right now, because your logic is clouded by your desires. Intelligent Mercury retrogrades between the Earth and the Sun on **September 3**, aligning your thoughts with a true sense of purpose. This conjunction is in your 2nd House of Values, so you're driven to explain where you stand on a key issue. But social Venus harmonizes with illusory Neptune on **September 4**, distorting your common sense and bending your words with subtle emotional content to communicate what you want instead of what you know. Stick with the facts to stay out of trouble.

SUPER NOVA DAYS

★ **SEPTEMBER 7–9**
pursuit of happiness
An uncomfortable quincunx from caring Venus to independent Uranus and overconfident Jupiter on **September 7–8** has you avoiding

109

intimacy one moment and pursuing it the next.
Venus's entry into passionate Scorpio on
September 8 and Jupiter's entry in compassionate Pisces on **September 9** further irks
you by requiring you to acknowledge your feelings, even if they don't support your goals.
Meanwhile, the discerning Virgo New Moon
suggests that practical logic will prevail, giving
you the direction you seek.

★ **SEPTEMBER 12–14**
wearing your heart on your sleeve
Messenger Mercury's direct turn on
September 12 usually allows you to discuss
what's on your mind. But reckless Mars forms
over reactive quincunxes with Uranus and
Jupiter in your 8th House of Intimacy on
September 13, so you could easily offend
someone you like by revealing too much, too
fast. When Mars enters secretive Scorpio and
your 4th House of Security on **September 14**,
you are reminded once again that you
can't expect others to cater to the needs of
your heart.

★ **SEPTEMBER 21**
lucky guess
Your life lights up from the Sun's brilliant
opposition to lucky Jupiter and electrifying
Uranus. Although you may need to handle a
financial problem—or at a minimum take care
of overdue bills—your perceptions are right on
the money, and you should be able to rise to
the task. Just avoid becoming a Pollyanna, for
you could inadvertently let an important dead-
line slip by if you blithely assume all will turn
out for the best.

★ **SEPTEMBER 30**
shoulder to the wheel
The Sun's annual conjunction with show stop-
ping Saturn arrives today in your 3rd House of
Immediate Environment, where it creates
obstacles in your everyday life. Saturn
restrains the expression of your heart energy
in order to sustain it over a longer period
of time. Instead of blaming external events
that get in your way, it's time to develop the
discipline reach your goals.

OCTOBER

METAPHORICAL
SECURITY BLANKET

Unexpected good news can spin you around and start your month off with a boost as Mercury opposes benevolent Jupiter and eye-opening Uranus on **October 1–2**. All in all, though, this is a rather somber time. Brainy Mercury enters reflective Libra and your 3rd House of Communication on **October 3**, joining serious Saturn there on **October 8**. Measure your words carefully and say exactly what you mean.

Additionally, the objective Libra New Moon on **October 7** falls in your data-rich 3rd House, presenting you with opposing viewpoints. It's tempting to favor one perspective over the other, yet the lesson of the Scales is to seek balance by giving each side equal consideration. Saturn's weight of responsibility may leave you feeling oppressed, but you can't just walk away from a tough situation. Your passions run rampant with both magnetic Venus and forceful Mars in profound Scorpio, tracking together through your 4th House of Home and Family.

Your attachment to the past is unsettling yet hard to release, for Venus turns retrograde on **October 8**, holding an awkward sesquisquare to rebellious Uranus throughout the first half of the month. You feel conflicted as you are attracted to the idea of breaking free while also taking solace from nostalgic memories. Mercury's entry into Scorpio and your 4th House on **October 20**, followed by the Sun on **October 23**, continues the retrospective theme. The spontaneous-spirited Aries Full Moon on **October 22** falls in your 9th House of Adventure, which can temporarily snap you back into the present. Nevertheless, your vision of the future is blurred by a long-term connection between realistic Saturn and fantasy-driven Neptune that is exact on **October 27**.

KEEP IN MIND THIS MONTH

Hard as it is to see the potential in every difficult situation, your positive thinking can have more power than you realize.

KEY DATES

★ **OCTOBER 1–3**
simple twist of fate
Someone may offer you a lucrative opportunity when communicator Mercury in your 2nd House of Money is aided by generous Jupiter on **October 1**. But it's not what you expect— and you could learn the rest of the story on **October 2** when radical Uranus enters the picture. Seductive Venus joins aggressive Mars on **October 3**, but your attempts to influence others will make the outcome more unpredictable than you can imagine.

SUPER NOVA DAYS

★ **OCTOBER 5–8**
surge of diplomacy
If you're being coerced to do something against your will, you'll resist with great intensity when trickster Mercury squares domineering Pluto on **October 5**. Although this can stir up a nasty conflict, Mercury is clever enough to help you talk your way out without having to fight. The New Moon in diplomatic

Libra on **October 7** adds finesse to your inter-personal toolbox, while Mercury's hookup with authoritative Saturn the next day gives you the clout to use your words effectively. Don't be afraid to tell it like it is, for others will look up to you as long as you keep your integrity and don't lose your cool.

★ **OCTOBER 16–18**
active listening

Discuss your plans with others on **October 16**, when interactive Mercury aligns with the will-ful Sun in your 3rd House of Information. But you're likely less interested in telling everyone what's on your mind than you are in having a dialogue and seeing their points of view. An intuitive Mercury-Neptune trine on **October 18** heightens your sensitivity and allows you to get to the true meaning of the message. Be sure to establish healthy boundaries, or you could become so enamored with someone else's perspective that you lose your own.

★ **OCTOBER 19–20**
unnecessary extravagance
Let caution be your watchword on **October 19**:
The Sun's trine to dreamy Neptune and healing Chiron in your 7th House of Partners
makes it so easy to see a situation through
other people's eyes, you have trouble negotiat-
ing for what you want. Action-hero Mars trines
magnanimous Jupiter in your 8th House of
Shared Resources on **October 20**, further
encouraging you to give too much away. Being
generous is one thing, but going overboard
with lavish offers isn't helpful to you in the
long run.

★ **OCTOBER 27–28**
energetic shifts
You're discouraged and disappointed in others
when somber Saturn forms an uneasy connection with ethereal Neptune on **October 27**,
making it hard to know what's real. Fortunately,
you can shake the malaise when spunky Mars
enters inspirational Sagittarius and your 5th
House of Play on **October 28**.

NOVEMBER

LET THE GOOD TIMES ROLL

It's time to lighten up your life. The transformative power of the Scorpio New Moon in your 4th House of Foundations on **November 6** motivates you to confront a lingering, unresolved hurt from the past—then let go of it and move on. Impulsive Mars in adventurous Sagittarius, a fellow fire sign, is now visiting your 5th House of Self-Expression, empowering you to do what makes you feel good in the moment.

Retrograde Venus—which polarizes your feelings while in fixed Scorpio—backs up into peaceful Libra and your 3rd House of Information on **November 7**. Although you've been revisiting issues tied to family dynamics or romantic involvements since Venus turned retrograde on **October 8**, your need for harmony in relationships now becomes more important than your drive for understanding. Chatty Mercury follows Mars into inspirational Sagittarius and your fun-loving 5th House on **November 8**, giving your words an uplifting and philosophical tilt. Then, when Venus turns direct along with philosophical Jupiter on **November 18**, you're able to say good-bye to a

previous attachment—a person or a dream—
without animosity or grief.

Your heart continues to open as you receive a
creative boost from the Mercury-Mars conjunction
on **November 20**. The determined Taurus Full
Moon on **November 21** reflects your unyielding
desire to bring the recent changes to fruition. By
the time the Sun enters confident Sagittarius on
November 22, the upcoming holiday season suddenly seems very near. Optimism continues to
replace caution through the end of the month, yet
cozy Venus's reentry into your private 4th House
on **November 29** encourages you to enjoy your
friends and family while staying close to home.

KEEP IN MIND THIS MONTH

*The shift may not be as quick as you wish, but recent
emotional storms are passing, leaving room
for some pleasure.*

KEY DATES

★ **NOVEMBER 4-6**
through the looking glass
Although the New Moon in shadowy Scorpio on
November 6 can put you in touch with complex
feelings, it's also a signal that a metamorphosis is under way. Rational Mercury's trines to
extravagant Jupiter on **November 4** and to
surprising Uranus on **November 6** bring good
news out of the blue. You're thrilled—perhaps
a little prematurely. Everything is not exactly
as it appears, for Mercury also squares mythi-
cal Neptune, pitting your logic against your
imagination. Setting aside time to lose yourself
in your dreams can help you stay grounded.

★ **NOVEMBER 15**
look beyond the horizon
You are gifted with extraordinary vision today:
The Sun in your 4th House of Security acts like
a superconductor for Jupiter's expansiveness
when these two giants form a harmonious
trine. This isn't just blind optimism, for
assertive Mars receives a reality check—along

with organizational assistance—from a sextile
to hardworking Saturn in your 3rd House of
Communication. By consciously reaching past
your comfort zone now, you can accomplish
more than you expect.

SUPER NOVA DAYS

★ **NOVEMBER 18–22**
closer to free
A little vacation from your mundane life may
not be such a bad idea. Just don't let your fantasies get out of hand on **November 18**, when
illusory Neptune is accentuated by aspects
from the self-centered Sun and trickster
Mercury. You can convince yourself that your
dreams are real, so be careful about making
any important decisions. But don't suppress
your urge to display your creativity, especially
as the Sun trines inventive Uranus on
November 19 and Mercury conjuncts fun-
loving Mars in your expressive 5th House
on **November 20**. The Taurus Full Moon on
November 21 falls in your 10th House of
Career, flooding your mind with practical ways
to complete your current work so you can

move on. When the Sun enters bold Sagittarius on **November 22**, you're already eager for the adventures ahead.

★ **NOVEMBER 27–30**
the sky's the limit
You have so many new ideas, you can't decide which to pursue when clever Mercury squares unconventional Uranus on **November 27**. Go ahead and take one of your strokes of brilliance as far as you can—and then a bit farther—when just-do-it Mars squares wildly enthusiastic Jupiter on **November 29**. Nevertheless, brace yourself for the serious planning and consistent hard work that must follow when Mercury enters tenacious Capricorn and your 6th House of Daily Routines on **November 30**.

DECEMBER

RIGHT AT THE EDGE

You often thrive on the holiday season, Leo—but this year you may lose steam as the month unfolds. The cheerful Sagittarius New Moon on **December 5** in your 5th House of Fun and Games encourages you to minimize serious issues that lurk behind the upcoming celebrations. Still, with smart Mercury conjoined defiant Pluto, you may believe that your good intentions can carry you right through to your goals. Yet your daily routine becomes more demanding when physical Mars enters structured Capricorn and your 6th House of Work and Service on **December 7**. Then as Mercury—also in Capricorn and your 6th House— turns retrograde on **December 10** to reconnect with Pluto on **December 13**, your plans may start to unravel. Brute force is tempting but unwise; this is a call to use your intelligence to increase your efficiency. The breakthrough you've been seeking probably won't occur until **January 4, 2011**, when opportunistic Jupiter joins brilliant Uranus for the third and final conjunction in a series that began on **June 8** and repeated on **September 18**.

Retrograde Mercury backs into easygoing
Sagittarius and your playful 5th House on
December 18, stimulating enjoyable discussions
more about pleasure than productivity. When the
Gemini Full Moon Eclipse on **December 21** falls
in your 11th House of Friends, social plans can
undergo radical revision at the last minute.
Additionally, this is the Winter Solstice, and
the Sun steps into traditional Capricorn to shift
your priorities away from self-expression toward
serving others. Be careful: Mercury's square
to outlandish Jupiter could encourage you to
promise more than you're willing to deliver. If
you do overcommit, get ready to backpedal on
December 29, when just-do-it Mars crosses
paths with judgmental Saturn.

KEEP IN MIND THIS MONTH

*You're on the edge of a significant shift, yet everything
takes longer than you expect. Instead of worrying, use
the additional time to perfect your plans.*

KEY DATES

★ **DECEMBER 1-5**
off to a great start
A whimsical thought can set you off on an adventure, but by **December 3** your plan gets out of hand: Mars's square to shocking Uranus suddenly changes everything. Fortunately, your mind is sharp, and your perceptions are so penetrating that you can have it all back in shape by the free-spirited Sagittarius New Moon on **December 5**.

★ **DECEMBER 13**
be the change
You're driven to make positive adjustments to your diet and lifestyle—even if it means enter- ing unfamiliar territory—when a triple con- junction of rational Mercury, courageous Mars, and incisive Pluto falls in your 6th House of Daily Routines on **December 13**. Just don't for- get that Mercury is in its trickster retrograde phase. You could be convinced you're doing the right thing when in fact you're just making matters worse. If you find yourself in an

intense struggle, back down graciously instead
of fighting to the finish.

★ **DECEMBER 16–18**
sunny-side up
An uplifting few days can be just what you need
to feel better about yourself, yet the contrast
between your fantasies and reality can still get
you down. The Sun's connection to hopeful
Jupiter on **December 16** allows you to extend
your vision beyond the immediate situations
that demand your attention. You may feel as if
you're returning to your past when retrograde
Mercury reenters your creative 5th House on
December 18, but this transit also brings
relief—especially if you're willing to let go of your
fixed views and roll with the changes announced
by the Sun's square with dynamic Uranus.

SUPER NOVA DAYS

★ **DECEMBER 20–21**
let the show begin
You're ready for fun yet challenged to keep
everything in line when rational Mercury gets
struck by the mind-opening Uranus-Jupiter

conjunction. But on **December 21**, the Full
Moon Eclipse and the Winter Solstice coincide,
reminding you that it's crucial to look ahead:
Big changes are just around the corner. Lean
on your friends for the support you need as
your life radically shifts.

★ **DECEMBER 26–30**
one more river to cross
No matter how strongly you feel about what
you're doing, try to moderate your intensity on
December 26 when the Sun joins relentless
Pluto. Don't deny your desires; just be aware
that you can inadvertently offend or frighten
someone with your passion. If you do come on
too strong, the Mars-Saturn square will show
you where you need to pull back by **December 29**.
Fortunately, Mercury turns direct on
December 30. Look for freer expression
and smoother sailing ahead.

APPENDIXES

★

2010 MONTH-AT-A-GLANCE ASTROCALENDAR

★

FAMOUS LEOS

★

LEO IN LOVE

FRIDAY 1 ★ You're raring to go, but potent forces slow you

SATURDAY 2 ★

SUNDAY 3 ★

MONDAY 4 ★

TUESDAY 5 ★

WEDNESDAY 6

THURSDAY 7

FRIDAY 8

SATURDAY 9

SUNDAY 10

MONDAY 11

TUESDAY 12

WEDNESDAY 13 ★ Pay close attention to your daily routine now

THURSDAY 14 ★

FRIDAY 15 ★ ●

SATURDAY 16

SUNDAY 17 ★ You see far into your future during these transitional days

MONDAY 18 ★

TUESDAY 19 ★

WEDNESDAY 20

THURSDAY 21

FRIDAY 22 ★ Formalizing a partnership is a wise move with lasting value

SATURDAY 23 ★

SUNDAY 24 ★

MONDAY 25

TUESDAY 26

WEDNESDAY 27 ★ **SUPER NOVA DAYS** A conflict exposes your true intentions

THURSDAY 28 ★

FRIDAY 29 ★

SATURDAY 30 ★ ○

SUNDAY 31 ★

★ designates key date

MONDAY 1	
TUESDAY 2	
WEDNESDAY 3	
THURSDAY 4	
FRIDAY 5 ★ Prepare for confusion	

SATURDAY 6 ★	
SUNDAY 7	
MONDAY 8	
TUESDAY 9	

WEDNESDAY 10 ★ **SUPER NOVA DAYS** Take care not to start an unnecessary fight by insisting you have all the answers

THURSDAY 11 ★	
FRIDAY 12 ★	
SATURDAY 13 ★ ●	
SUNDAY 14	
MONDAY 15 ★ You receive mixed messages from someone close to you	

TUESDAY 16 ★	
WEDNESDAY 17	
THURSDAY 18	
FRIDAY 19	
SATURDAY 20	
SUNDAY 21	
MONDAY 22	
TUESDAY 23	
WEDNESDAY 24	
THURSDAY 25	
FRIDAY 26	
SATURDAY 27 ★ Let go of your need to rationalize your ideas	

SUNDAY 28 ★ ○

MONDAY 1 ★ Take a plunge into the unknown, but expect the unexpected

TUESDAY 2 ★

WEDNESDAY 3 ★

THURSDAY 4

FRIDAY 5

SATURDAY 6

SUNDAY 7 ★ Ask for your heart's desire, but behave responsibly

MONDAY 8 ★

TUESDAY 9 ★

WEDNESDAY 10

THURSDAY 11

FRIDAY 12

SATURDAY 13

SUNDAY 14

MONDAY 15 ★ ● SUPER NOVA DAYS Lightning strikes, and your words gain force

TUESDAY 16 ★

WEDNESDAY 17 ★

THURSDAY 18 ★

FRIDAY 19

SATURDAY 20

SUNDAY 21 ★ Yes morphs into no right before your eyes

MONDAY 22 ★

TUESDAY 23

WEDNESDAY 24

THURSDAY 25 ★ You face a formidable—and resourceful—opponent at work

FRIDAY 26

SATURDAY 27

SUNDAY 28

MONDAY 29 ○

TUESDAY 30

WEDNESDAY 31

THURSDAY 1 ★ Magic is in the air, unleashing the power of change

FRIDAY 2

SATURDAY 3 ★ Uneasy romantic attractions are stirred today

SUNDAY 4 ★

MONDAY 5 ★

TUESDAY 6 ★

WEDNESDAY 7

THURSDAY 8

FRIDAY 9

SATURDAY 10 ★ You struggle to be true to yourself without angering others

SUNDAY 11

MONDAY 12

TUESDAY 13

WEDNESDAY 14 ●

THURSDAY 15

FRIDAY 16

SATURDAY 17 ★ You see the silver lining in every dark cloud today

SUNDAY 18 ★

MONDAY 19 ★

TUESDAY 20

WEDNESDAY 21

THURSDAY 22

FRIDAY 23 ★ SUPER NOVA DAYS Everything in your life is stretched to the max

SATURDAY 24 ★

SUNDAY 25 ★

MONDAY 26 ★

TUESDAY 27

WEDNESDAY 28 ○

THURSDAY 29

FRIDAY 30

SATURDAY 1

SUNDAY 2 ★ Despite your frustration, it's important to express feelings without emotional drama

MONDAY 3 ★

TUESDAY 4 ★

WEDNESDAY 5

THURSDAY 6

FRIDAY 7

SATURDAY 8

SUNDAY 9

MONDAY 10 ★ An unpleasant power struggle is brewing at work

TUESDAY 11 ★

WEDNESDAY 12 ★

THURSDAY 13 ★ ●

FRIDAY 14

SATURDAY 15

SUNDAY 16

MONDAY 17 ★ **SUPER NOVA DAYS** Finances may turn problematic

TUESDAY 18 ★

WEDNESDAY 19 ★

THURSDAY 20 ★

FRIDAY 21

SATURDAY 22

SUNDAY 23

MONDAY 24

TUESDAY 25

WEDNESDAY 26

THURSDAY 27 ★ O You are on the edge of a very exciting time in your life

FRIDAY 28

SATURDAY 29

SUNDAY 30

MONDAY 31

TUESDAY 1 ★ Don't be afraid to take a chance to radically change your life

WEDNESDAY 2 ★

THURSDAY 3

FRIDAY 4 ★ **SUPER NOVA DAYS** Try to keep your balance during
an exciting whirlwind

SATURDAY 5 ★

SUNDAY 6 ★

MONDAY 7 ★

TUESDAY 8 ★

WEDNESDAY 9

THURSDAY 10 ★ Your mental chatter increases, causing a distraction

FRIDAY 11 ★

SATURDAY 12 ★ ●

SUNDAY 13

MONDAY 14

TUESDAY 15

WEDNESDAY 16

THURSDAY 17

FRIDAY 18

SATURDAY 19 ★ Don't expect much rest; important decisions need
to be made

SUNDAY 20 ★

MONDAY 21 ★

TUESDAY 22 ★

WEDNESDAY 23 ★

THURSDAY 24

FRIDAY 25 ★ Instability grows, but things will settle down soon

SATURDAY 26 ★ ○

SUNDAY 27

MONDAY 28

TUESDAY 29

WEDNESDAY 30

THURSDAY 1 ★ Sharing a dream is the clearest way to express what you want

FRIDAY 2 ★

SATURDAY 3 ★

SUNDAY 4

MONDAY 5

TUESDAY 6

WEDNESDAY 7

THURSDAY 8 ★ Don't make any long-term relationship or fiscal decisions yet

FRIDAY 9 ★

SATURDAY 10 ★

SUNDAY 11 ★ ●

MONDAY 12

TUESDAY 13 ★ Wealth could be elusive today

WEDNESDAY 14

THURSDAY 15

FRIDAY 16

SATURDAY 17

SUNDAY 18

MONDAY 19

TUESDAY 20

WEDNESDAY 21

THURSDAY 22 ★ Sound judgment and hard work will ensure good results

FRIDAY 23 ★

SATURDAY 24

SUNDAY 25 ★ ○ **SUPER NOVA DAYS** Be cautious if an authority resists your plans

MONDAY 26 ★

TUESDAY 27

WEDNESDAY 28

THURSDAY 29

FRIDAY 30

SATURDAY 31

SUNDAY 1

MONDAY 2

TUESDAY 3 ★ Consciously curbing your intensity can prevent future problems

WEDNESDAY 4 ★

THURSDAY 5

FRIDAY 6

SATURDAY 7 ★ Extreme behavior triggers intense reactions

SUNDAY 8 ★

MONDAY 9 ★ ●

TUESDAY 10 ★

WEDNESDAY 11

THURSDAY 12

FRIDAY 13 ★ Emotional breakthroughs in relationships could begin now

SATURDAY 14 ★

SUNDAY 15 ★

MONDAY 16 ★

TUESDAY 17

WEDNESDAY 18

THURSDAY 19

FRIDAY 20 ★ SUPER NOVA DAYS You are forced to reevaluate all your plans

SATURDAY 21 ★

SUNDAY 22

MONDAY 23

TUESDAY 24 ★ ○ You must let go of the past and bravely move on

WEDNESDAY 25 ★

THURSDAY 26 ★

FRIDAY 27

SATURDAY 28

SUNDAY 29

MONDAY 30

TUESDAY 31

WEDNESDAY 1

THURSDAY 2

FRIDAY 3 ★ Stick with the facts to stay out of trouble

SATURDAY 4 ★

SUNDAY 5

MONDAY 6

TUESDAY 7 ★ SUPER NOVA DAYS You avoid intimacy one moment and pursue it the next

WEDNESDAY 8 ★ ●

THURSDAY 9 ★

FRIDAY 10

SATURDAY 11

SUNDAY 12 ★ You could offend someone by revealing too much, too fast

MONDAY 13 ★

TUESDAY 14 ★

WEDNESDAY 15

THURSDAY 16

FRIDAY 17

SATURDAY 18

SUNDAY 19

MONDAY 20

TUESDAY 21 ★ You may need to handle a financial problem

WEDNESDAY 22

THURSDAY 23 ○

FRIDAY 24

SATURDAY 25

SUNDAY 26

MONDAY 27

TUESDAY 28

WEDNESDAY 29

THURSDAY 30 ★ Don't be a slave to circumstance

FRIDAY 1 ★ Someone may offer you a lucrative opportunity

SATURDAY 2 ★

SUNDAY 3 ★

MONDAY 4

TUESDAY 5 ★ **SUPER NOVA DAYS** Don't be afraid to tell it like it is

WEDNESDAY 6 ★

THURSDAY 7 ★ ●

FRIDAY 8 ★

SATURDAY 9

SUNDAY 10

MONDAY 11

TUESDAY 12

WEDNESDAY 13

THURSDAY 14

FRIDAY 15

SATURDAY 16 ★ You are more interested in other points of view now

SUNDAY 17 ★

MONDAY 18 ★

TUESDAY 19 ★ Let caution be your watchword

WEDNESDAY 20 ★

THURSDAY 21

FRIDAY 22 ○

SATURDAY 23

SUNDAY 24

MONDAY 25

TUESDAY 26

WEDNESDAY 27 ★ You find it hard to know what's real

THURSDAY 28 ★

FRIDAY 29

SATURDAY 30

SUNDAY 31

MONDAY 1

TUESDAY 2

WEDNESDAY 3

THURSDAY 4 ★ Unexpected good news incites a premature celebration

FRIDAY 5 ★

SATURDAY 6 ★ ●

SUNDAY 7

MONDAY 8

TUESDAY 9

WEDNESDAY 10

THURSDAY 11

FRIDAY 12

SATURDAY 13

SUNDAY 14

MONDAY 15 ★ You are gifted with extraordinary vision today

TUESDAY 16

WEDNESDAY 17

THURSDAY 18 ★ **SUPER NOVA DAYS** A little vacation from your mundane life is not a bad idea

FRIDAY 19 ★

SATURDAY 20 ★

SUNDAY 21 ★ ○

MONDAY 22 ★

TUESDAY 23

WEDNESDAY 24

THURSDAY 25

FRIDAY 26

SATURDAY 27 ★ Take one of your strokes of brilliance as far as you can

SUNDAY 28 ★

MONDAY 29 ★

TUESDAY 30 ★

WEDNESDAY 1 ★ Your sharp mind will help you confront a sudden change

THURSDAY 2 ★

FRIDAY 3 ★

SATURDAY 4 ★

SUNDAY 5 ★ ●

MONDAY 6

TUESDAY 7

WEDNESDAY 8

THURSDAY 9

FRIDAY 10

SATURDAY 11

SUNDAY 12

MONDAY 13 ★ You're driven to make positive diet and lifestyle adjustments

TUESDAY 14

WEDNESDAY 15

THURSDAY 16 ★ Let go of your fixed views and roll with the changes

FRIDAY 17 ★

SATURDAY 18 ★

SUNDAY 19

MONDAY 20 ★ **SUPER NOVA DAYS** Lean on friends for support as your life radically shifts

TUESDAY 21 ★ ○

WEDNESDAY 22

THURSDAY 23

FRIDAY 24

SATURDAY 25

SUNDAY 26 ★ Don't deny your desires, but don't come on too strong

MONDAY 27 ★

TUESDAY 28 ★

WEDNESDAY 29 ★

THURSDAY 30 ★

FRIDAY 31

FAMOUS LEOS

Nomar Garciaparra	★	7/23/1973
Slash	★	7/23/1965
Amelia Earhart	★	7/24/1897
Jennifer Lopez	★	7/24/1970
Simón Bolívar	★	7/24/1783
Zelda Fitzgerald	★	7/24/1900
Alexandre Dumas	★	7/24/1802
George Bernard Shaw	★	7/26/1856
Aldous Huxley	★	7/26/1894
Stanley Kubrick	★	7/26/1928
Mick Jagger	★	7/26/1943
Dorothy Hamill	★	7/26/1956
Kevin Spacey	★	7/26/1959
Sandra Bullock	★	7/26/1964
Peggy Fleming	★	7/27/1948
Beatrix Potter	★	7/28/1866
Jacqueline Kennedy Onassis	★	7/28/1929
Stanley Kunitz	★	7/29/1905
Peter Jennings	★	7/29/1938
Emily Brontë	★	7/30/1818
Henry Ford	★	7/30/1863
Buddy Guy	★	7/30/1936
Peter Bogdanovich	★	7/30/1939
Arnold Schwarzenegger	★	7/30/1947
Hilary Swank	★	7/30/1974
J. K. Rowling	★	7/31/1965
Herman Melville	★	8/1/1819
Francis Scott Key	★	8/1/1779
Jerry Garcia	★	8/1/1942
James Baldwin	★	8/2/1924
Martha Stewart	★	8/3/1941
Martin Sheen	★	8/3/1940
Tom Brady	★	8/3/1977
Louis Armstrong	★	8/4/1901
Jeff Gordon	★	8/4/1971

FAMOUS LEOS

Neil Armstrong	★	8/5/1930
Lucille Ball	★	8/6/1911
Andy Warhol	★	8/6/1928
Charlize Theron	★	8/7/1975
Louis Leakey	★	8/7/1903
Esther Williams	★	8/8/1922
Dustin Hoffman	★	8/8/1937
Whitney Houston	★	8/9/1963
Herbert Hoover	★	8/10/1874
Antonio Banderas	★	8/10/1960
Reverend Jerry Falwell	★	8/11/1933
Hulk Hogan	★	8/11/1953
Pete Sampras	★	8/12/1971
George Hamilton	★	8/12/1939
Annie Oakley	★	8/13/1860
Alfred Hitchcock	★	8/13/1899
Danielle Steel	★	8/14/1947
Halle Berry	★	8/14/1968
Earvin "Magic" Johnson	★	8/14/1959
Napoléon Bonaparte	★	8/15/1769
Ben Affleck	★	8/15/1972
Charles Bukowski	★	8/16/1920
Madonna	★	8/16/1958
Angela Bassett	★	8/16/1958
Mae West	★	8/17/1893
Robert De Niro	★	8/17/1943
Roman Polanski	★	8/18/1933
Robert Redford	★	8/18/1937
Bill Clinton	★	8/19/1946
H. P. Lovecraft	★	8/20/1890
Jacqueline Susann	★	8/20/1918
Connie Chung	★	8/20/1946
Robert Plant	★	8/20/1948
Joe Strummer	★	8/21/1952
Kim Cattrall	★	8/21/1956
Wilt Chamberlain	★	8/21/1936
Dorothy Parker	★	8/22/1893

LEO IN LOVE

LEO–ARIES (MARCH 21–APRIL 19)

Glorious Leo! Your sign is ruled by the brilliant Sun and you tend to be creative and generous. You live to love and be loved. You relish basking in the limelight. You're much more vulnerable than others know; your cheerful disposition and self-confidence is often misleading. If your love isn't returned with adoration you'll eventually retreat. When you team up with an Aries, you two fire signs can have lots of fun stirring up all kinds of enjoyment. If, however, your Moon is in an earth sign, you'll tend to sacrifice pleasure for stability, which may scare off your impulsive Ram. You both maintain a youthful attitude toward life and are exuberant when you're in love. But your Aries playmate can quickly tire of most any game, and it will be important for you to keep new tricks up your sleeve. You tend to be more loyal than the Ram, and it can be disconcerting to you when he or she does not follow through on promises. Aries can be as self-centered and demanding as you; so you will both need to balance your needs so each of you can take turns being the star. All in all, this is a high-spirited, passionate match worth pursuing.

LEO–TAURUS (APRIL 20–MAY 20)

You're one of the four fixed signs of the zodiac, along with Taurus, Scorpio, and Aquarius. When you meet up with another strong individual such as a Taurus, you'll each have to learn to give and take within the boundaries of the relationship. You have a big and tender heart, giving generously to your partner as long as you're receiving plenty of love and affection in return. Your Taurus lover seeks simple pleasures and can be very sensual. The Bull is ruled by the planet Venus, which places a tremendous emphasis on the value of love. The two of you come together with a strong sense of love already established within. The work is to become receptive and open to each other's needs. In this way, both of your unique ways of sharing affection can be readily accepted by each other. You need a lot of attention. Taurus needs a lot of touch. You both have the capacity for unwavering loyalty in love, but you can each be also quite stubborn in your own ways. Without relief from harmonious placements of the Moon, Venus, or Mars, your relationship can turn into a battleground. If you can get past your own self-interests and learn to give freely to your Bull, this can be a dynamic match with lots of material abundance and goodwill.

LEO–GEMINI (MAY 21–JUNE 20)

Your naturally sunny disposition gives you charisma that lights up any room. You can be very personable, as long as you feel that you are receiving your fair share of recognition. You readily share center stage with others as long as you get to be the lead. Your Gemini partner is motivated by communication, and you can be entranced by your lover's charm, wit, and delightful banter. When you are in a relationship with Gemini, a powerful, magnetic attraction takes place that lifts both of your spirits and heightens your mutual curiosity about each other and the world. You make great playmates, in life, at work, or in bed. Creative sparks fly if you learn to play well and respect each other's need for attention and approval. If your Venus is in Virgo, you think your Gemini friend is a bit too scattered. If your Venus is in Cancer, he or she may be a bit too noisy for you. But with your Venus in Gemini or Leo, you will experience a loving bond. The bottom line is that you may not be as natural with language as your lover is, but as a talented performer, you really know how to put on a show. Together, you can be extremely creative and productive, while having more than your fair share of fun along the way.

LEO-CANCER (JUNE 21–JULY 22)

You tend to direct your energy outward and may be considered extroverted. You are less inclined to consider the needs of others as much as your Cancer friend. Your bright, sunny ways may have to be adjusted to consider the emotions of moody Cancer, who is often introverted, pensive, and attuned to others' feelings. In a way, you're like day and night. You're the Sun. Your lover is the Moon. It will take some time for you two to adjust to your differences, but it will be easier if the Moon in your birth chart is in Cancer or another water sign, like Scorpio or Pisces. Regardless, you demand attention and need daily approval and affirmation. You can easily outshine Cancer, who requires less attention and demonstrative affection. The most important thing for your quiet Cancer sweetheart is that he or she needs to be secure in an intimate relationship. You must ask yourself if you have the ability to give this kind of healing devotion. You'll need to offer each other plenty of room to express yourselves, while at the same time paying close attention to each others' needs. This can be a difficult relationship unless, for the sake of peace at home, you are willing to turn your loud roar into a quiet purr.

LEO-LEO (JULY 23–AUGUST 22)

When the same sun signs join together, there is a possibility for growth and self-reflection for both individuals. You Leos need plenty of affirmation from the world around you. When two Lions unite, there may be some posturing and roaring as you compete for attention. One of you will want to be the alpha cat, but you're going to need to share the leading role. If you each can remain good-natured, laugh at your own quirks, and compliment each other, then you stand a good chance for success. You are a creative soul and feel that you're special. It is difficult to confine your life to stringent rules. Put two of you together and you'll quickly learn how to cope with one another's tendency toward arrogance and pride, or the relationship will self-destruct. You will both need to keep your claws retracted when you fight, or someone will get hurt. If either or both of you have the Moon in a more receptive earth or water sign, then you'll be more compatible. Underneath your apparent self-confidence is a layer of vulnerability. You and your Leo mate must stay aware of how you can help each other with this sensitive personality trait. This relationship can be fantastic if you can get past the ego and control issues.

LEO-VIRGO (AUGUST 23–SEPT. 22)

When you meet a Virgo, you quickly realize that many of your gregarious actions are up for judgment and ridicule under Virgo's critical eye. This level of discernment can make you very uncomfortable—causing you to become more vulnerable than you'd like in the presence of Virgo's analysis. Your Virgo partner prefers to assume the upper edge of power in relationships, and will use their sharp intellect to efficiently take what power they can. If your Venus or Mars is in the sign of Cancer, this will ease the situation. It's an interesting problem, for you seem to be more proactive, yet Virgo holds the cards. If you are as clever as a Lion should be, you'll find a multitude of ways to humor your Virgo. Underneath a veil of judgment, he or she is extremely witty and funny, with a keen sense of humor. You may feel pressure from your mate to perform perfectly, but it's probably not as important as your attitude. Once you settle on a harmonious balance of power within this relationship, you'll be able to help each other quite a lot. Your Virgo lover helps perfect that which your exuberance creates. You can really fire up your Virgo, and if the two of you don't end up in love, at least you make good business partners.

LEO-LIBRA (SEPT. 23–OCT. 22)

Your charismatic personality is outwardly bright and naturally endowed with humor, drama, and colorful dress. You love beauty, ornate costumes, and entertaining friends and family with your generosity. Libra is the detached connoisseur of good taste and prefers refined modes of décor. However, you both admire the qualities of each other's artistic skill. Your Libra lover may not fully approve of your many masks and antics. On the other hand, you just might find your classy Libra a bit too stuffy. You jump in and get your hands dirty, but your partner would rather coach with their artful eye from the sidelines. You will have many things in common and can share theater, museums, and art classes. You will probably have distinctive styles that are quite different from each other. If Venus is in Libra in your chart or in Leo in your partner's chart, your styles may be more compatible. Your dress preference may serve as a metaphor for other aspects of behaviors and life patterns that distinguish the two of you from each other. Even with these differences, you can find contentment and happiness with a gracious Libra for a mate.

LEO–SCORPIO (OCT. 23–NOV. 21)

Both you and your Scorpio have strong personalities and are quite fixed in your individual ways. There will need to be enough attraction between the two of you to overcome the initial resistance you each may feel toward the other. Scorpios often find frolicking Leo a bit childish and difficult to understand, as they prefer their drama in private. They cherish boundaries and require more space in emotional situations than you do. You need dramatic and overt displays of affection that you may not get from your Scorpio lover, who is more reserved, resourceful, and careful of sharing deep feelings. If your Moon is in Scorpio or Taurus, then you are already in touch with this conflict between what is expressed and what is held in reserve, thereby taking the pressure off your Scorpio mate. The bottom line is that in order for this relationship to be successful, you need to learn how to be more introspective, while your lover makes a commitment to try to understand your need for attention. Given some common ground and support from a compatible Venus and Mars, you two can ignite an intense and long-lasting passion that can fill your heart with joy and that can remain sexy throughout the long haul.

LEO–SAGITTARIUS (NOV. 22–DEC. 21)

You can find love and happiness with an inspirational and adventurous Archer, but because you are both willing to live in the moment, you will probably need to have a strong Saturn contact between your charts to give you the glue of longevity. With or without aspects to Saturn, you make a fun and energetic pair. The two of you love to travel and learn about the diverse world around you, treating the world as your playground. The two of you could easily share interests in social events, sports, and adventures of all types. Your Sagittarius partner opens you to new and exciting vistas and helps you to move beyond the scope of personal interest toward a larger philosophical and global concern. You loyally offer your mate an enthusiastic path to explore his or her innate good nature and humor. The romantic exchange between you is easy and will keep your energy high-spirited and playful. This is a very good match that allows your passion to be expressed. The success of the relationship may depend upon your ability to create stability in the most basic practical realms of life.

LEO–CAPRICORN (DEC. 22–JAN. 19)

Your loving and charismatic disposition makes it easy for friends and family to applaud your efforts and creativity. Capricorns, on the other hand, with Saturn as their key planet, are serious individuals who can have a difficult time expressing themselves outwardly. Without compatible contacts between the Moon, Venus, or Mars in your individual charts, you'll feel like your Capricorn is raining on your parade. Regardless of other planets, usually conservative Capricorn will disapprove of your playful ways unless you're able to take full responsibility for your own well-being. If you can do that, then your Capricorn partner sees you as a valuable asset in his or her game plan to get ahead in life. Ultimately, both of you have self-interest in mind. You're aware of yourself as you observe your impact on others, while socially aware Capricorn is more interested in your external status as a couple. You may feel that you're being treated as a child and come to put your partner in a parental role. Be careful about creating this kind of possible detrimental dynamic. If you can learn the virtues of hard work and responsibility, your Capricorn will soften and incorporate more play into life—leading to a committed, successful relationship.

LEO-AQUARIUS [JAN. 20–FEB. 18]

Leo and Aquarius are two of the four fixed signs of the zodiac—representing a rigid, stubborn, and sometimes unyielding nature. You can be demanding and forceful if you don't get your way, demonstrating a childlike mentality as you defend yourself against imagined threats, no matter what the odds. It isn't that you need to be right as much as you need to be recognized and loved. You just want your Aquarian partner to appreciate you. The problem is that Aquarius is opposite Leo in the zodiac, and your intellectually oriented Aquarius mate takes pride in rational logic. He or she is much more interested in being right. So the two of you can go head to head, demanding, pleading, and lecturing each other. This may sound terrible, but it can be avoided if you remember two simple rules: You're ruled by the heart and need affection; your lover is ruled by the head and needs mental interaction. If the Moon in your chart is in an air sign, compatibility will be more easily within reach. Opposites do attract and, in this case, you and your mate are intrigued by each other and will be drawn into exploring the potential of a relationship. Compatibility isn't ensured, but you can make it work if you're both persevering and flexible.

LEO-PISCES [JAN. 20–FEB. 18]

Your outgoing and fiery nature may be easily confused by Pisces, who in turn can be baffled by your relentless self-expression and readiness for action. Compared to the Fish, your ego is strong. You shine with self-confidence and a larger-than-life personal grandeur. You tend to think of yourself first, even though you can be extremely generous with loved ones. On the other hand, your Pisces lover is not particularly inclined to put self-interest first. They tend to be compassionate, gentle, and typically avoid the spotlight. In some ways, you Lions are a complete mystery to the Fish, who experiences life under the seas of imagination and spirituality, and through the undercurrents of feelings and sensitivity. Your Pisces mate expresses his or her sensitivity by way of humility, while you express your vulnerability by way of your showy pride. You fend off potential attacks by roaring, while your Fishy friend fears being eaten alive by the Lion. If Venus in your chart is in Cancer or Virgo, you may be more mellow, and more compatible with your Pisces lover. In any case, you and your Pisces mate will need to find a genuine common ground from which to share your life if this is to be a solid and lasting union.

ABOUT THE AUTHORS

RICK LEVINE When I first encountered astrology as a psychology undergraduate in the late 1960s, I became fascinated with the varieties of human experience. Even now, I love the one-on-one work of seeing clients and looking at their lives through the cosmic lens. But I also love history and utilize astrology to better understand the longer-term cycles of cultural change. My recent DVD, *Quantum Astrology*, explores some of these transpersonal interests. As a scientist, I'm always looking for patterns in order to improve my ability to predict the outcome of any experiment; as an artist, I'm entranced by the mystery of what we do not and cannot know. As an astrologer, I am privileged to live in an enchanted world that links the rational and magical, physical and spiritual—and yes—even science and art.

JEFF JAWER I'm a Taurus with a Scorpio Moon and Aries rising who lives in the Pacific Northwest with Danick, my double-Pisces musician wife, our two Leo daughters, a black Gemini cat, and a white Pisces dog. I have been a professional astrologer since 1973 when I was a student at the University of Massachusetts (Amherst). I encountered astrology as my first marriage was ending and I was searching for answers. Astrology provided them. More than thirty-five years later, it remains the creative passion of my life as I continue to counsel, write, study, and share ideas with clients and colleagues around the world.

ACKNOWLEDGMENTS

Thanks to Paul O'Brien, our agent, our friend, and the creative genius behind Tarot.com; Gail Goldberg, the editor who always makes us sound better; Marcus Leaver and Michael Fragnito at Sterling Publishing, for their tireless support for the project; Barbara Berger, our supervising editor, who has shepherded this book with Taurean persistence and Aquarian invention; Laura Jorstad, for her refinement of the text; and Sterling project editor Mary Hern, editorial assistant Melanie Madden, and designer Gavin Motnyk for their invaluable help. We thank Bob Wietrak and Jules Herbert at Barnes & Noble, and all of the helping hands at Sterling. Thanks for the art and ideas from Jessica Abel and the rest of the Tarot.com team. Thanks as well to 3+Co. for the original design and to Tara Gimmer for the author photo.